Finding the

ORIGINATION POINT

Understanding Our Biases
to Create a More Peaceful World

Bill de la Cruz

© 2017 Bill de la Cruz

Special thanks to those who generously granted their permission to include their material in this book. All reasonable attempts have been made to obtain permission for the use of material quoted in the book. We regret any errors and omissions. If the owner of any material published in this book believes that such permission has not been granted, please contact us at: Legal@delacruzsolutions.com.

Information provided in this book is for informational purposes only and is not intended as professional advice. The author and publisher disclaim any responsibility for any liability, loss or risk incurred as a result, directly or indirectly, from the use of this book.

Names and identifying characteristics of individuals in this book have been changed.

Special thanks to the talented photographers who generously granted us permission to use their photos in this book. Special thanks to Boris H. Pophristov (pophristov.com), Will Dickey (willdickey.com), Erick Lohre (Erick Lohre Photography), Tina Schuler (tinaschuler.com), Andrew Kowalyshyn (AKPHOTO.com).

ISBN: 978-0-9995662-0-6
LCCN: 2017958691

Published by
Inner Wisdom Institute™ Programs, Colorado.
All rights reserved.

Conversations on Bias
Inner Wisdom Institute™
Workshops

Available now through www.delacruzsolutions.com

Printed in China

Table of Contents

"

As I explored myself, I realized that I was living a life that was hurtful and ego driven, and I had no one to blame except myself. It was mine to own.

> Throughout my life, I had created a collection of stories in my head that drove my behavior. A common thread in these stories was the ego-driven idea that I was a good and important person, and if there was a problem, it was the other person's problem.

Finding the

ORIGINATION POINT

Understanding Our Biases
to Create a More Peaceful World

Bill de la Cruz

Dedication

This book is dedicated to my grandson, Jackson, who continually reminds me about the importance of being happy, playful, and loving. Having a more humane and loving world for Jackson to grow up in is what inspires me to continue to do my own work.

"

"The journey of a thousand miles begins with a single step."

—Lao Tzu

Chapter 1

Daily Reflective Practice: Self-Assessment
The "Why"

Do you ever feel confused, unhappy, angry, or lost? Do you find yourself wondering how things ended up the way they are in your life? You are not alone. Throughout my life, I have had those same feelings and questions and wished I knew the steps to take to change myself and therefore my life circumstances. Without answers, I made up a lot of stories about my life, as we do. Not surprisingly, in my version of the story, I was always the good guy. My good guy reality was driven by the stories I told myself and not the factual reality of what was unfolding in front of me. The fact was, I was doing some damage in my life and to those around me by repeating cycles that were created by my stories.

When I realized the damage I was doing, I started to read a lot of books and went to a lot of workshops, as many do. The problem was, I still did not understand the steps to change. I was looking for a way to make every situation match my expectations without having to do any personal work to make that happen. I was living to make my reality match my expectations. I was so unskilled that I just made up story after story to explain away problems, and I was always the victim of circumstances.

> **I was so unskilled that I just made up story after story to explain away problems, and I was always the victim of circumstances.**

When our lived experiences do not meet our expectations, we tend to justify what is happening based on our perceptions and make up stories about what we are experiencing. The perceptions become our truth, which overrules the confusing reality of what is actually happening. Our expectations and reality are clashing to create the confusion we are experiencing.

We are all adept at creating stories and justifications for the many things that occur in our lives, especially when we feel things in our lives are out of control. The expectation is that because I am in charge, this is my life, and I know what to do to have it make sense! Right? I am in control! Or so I thought.

This idea that I was in control drove a large part of my life, and I learned in many ways that I was not in control at all. When I was growing up, my family was struggling with anger in our relationships, addiction, divorce, and the inability to communicate our feelings. Those dynamics were hard to face, so I made up a story about how great my life was and how it would all be good in the long run.

> **I thought I could tolerate all the negativity of my home life by pretending that my life was like that of the children in the television shows and that we had a happy family.**

The television shows I watched growing up were *Leave It to Beaver*, *Ozzie and Harriet*, and *The Jetsons*, which depicted families where the mom stayed home, happily cleaning and cooking in a dress, with high heels and makeup, while the husband went to work as the "breadwinner." Everyone returned home happy and sat around the table talking about their day. I thought that was how all real families got along.

I thought I could tolerate all the negativity of my home life by pretending that my life was like that of the children in the television shows and that we had a happy family. I told myself that if I worked hard enough, thought about it enough, and maintained enough control over my life, I could have that happy life shown on television. This was

> We are all adept at creating stories and justifications for the many things that occur in our lives, especially when we feel that things in our lives are out of control.

what I told myself, because my real life, the one I was covering up with my pretend life, was too hard to handle.

> **The only thing I knew for sure was that we were not living the life of the television family where everyone was portrayed as loving, communicative, and supportive.**

Reality hit me square in the face on May 24, 1969. I was 13 years old and sleeping in my room at home when the phone rang. It was before 6 a.m., so this was unusual, and I was startled out of my bed. As I walked into the kitchen, I saw my mom and heard her yelling into the phone to call the ambulance, call the fire department. I soon realized that my mom was talking to my sister Lee's boyfriend, and there was something wrong with my sister. I was standing close to my mom and the phone, and I heard her boyfriend say, "I think it's too late, she's cold."

My sister died in her sleep that night, one day shy of her 20th birthday. My ideas about life and my thoughts about who was in control were irreversibly changed. My entire family was devastated, and it was hard to talk about it without someone going into shame, blame, guilt, or anger. We all were both traumatized and unable to share our feelings.

At that time, the only thing I knew for sure was that we were not living the life of the television family where everyone was portrayed as loving, communicative, and supportive. I never saw anyone die on any of the happy family shows I watched growing up. My parents were not able to help themselves or their family because they lacked skills in communication and managing conflict as well as an understanding of the underlying issues our family had.

Little by little, my parents, my siblings, and I checked out of our family life. Our family was torn apart by abuse, lack of communication, death, and the inability to deal with the reality of our day-to-day circumstances. I had other personal issues that were woven into my life at this time, and I was also questioning who I was from a cultural and ethnic perspective.

After my sister died, I started questioning everything about who I was as a person. For my entire life, I had been told that I was white, but through my own questioning, I realized that was not true. I am Mexican, Spanish, and Native American. As a result, I had no understanding of who I really was and felt groundless and confused. Being raised as white meant that I had no cultural grounding in who I am ethnically and had only a false understanding of what it meant to be white. As a youth, being raised white was my reality, and I was angry when I understood that to be false. I used that story to add another level of justification for my behavior of being rude and self-centered, an angry, broken kid who felt it was easier to push someone away than to connect with people and be hurt again.

The culmination of my sister's death and my lack of cultural grounding shattered all of the ideas and ideals I had learned about myself up to this point. I did not take any responsibility for how I was feeling, and it became easy to blame other people for how I felt and what I was going through. Therefore, I lived much of my life as an angry person. As my behavior grew worse, I became more and more resistant to looking within.

> **My behavior and feelings were so ugly that I did not want to own them. I knew I was hurtful and demeaning to others ... because I was lashing out in an attempt to reduce my own pain.**

My behavior and feelings were so ugly that I did not want to own them. I knew I was hurtful and demeaning to others, without any care or consideration for how they felt because I was lashing out in an attempt to reduce my own pain.

The point of change for me came when I realized that my behavior was leading me down a path of self-destruction. I began to understand that my denial about my behavior was not serving me, and nothing in my life was getting better. As hard as the first step was, I knew that if I did not make that step to look at myself, my life would never change.

Starting this journey of self-reflection was the hardest step because the truth was that I did not like my thoughts, my behavior, or myself. My first step toward growth was to look within, examine my behavior, and see myself as others saw me. I had to be willing to explore the stories that I told myself about who I was and why I behaved the way I did.

Throughout my life, I had created a collection of stories in my head that drove my behavior. A common thread in these stories was the ego-driven idea that I was a good and important person, and if there was a problem, it was the other person's problem, because I was right and good. I lived this ego-driven way for the first half of my life, and for me this point of view was normal. Over time, it became very challenging to live this way, and I realized that I had to make changes in my life. As I became more aware, I started to look within and consciously change the ways I treated myself and other people.

I learned that in order to promote and sustain change, I would have to do my self-improvement work daily. To improve myself, I found that I had to be honest about where I currently was in my life. I had to accept myself for how I had been moving through my life and had to be brutally honest about the dysfunction in my thinking and behavior.

I understand now that the "work" of personal change is creating and committing to practices that I can do throughout my day and week, to help me become more aware of my feelings, thoughts, and actions. Committing to daily practices is key because the goal was and still is to grow my understanding of the consequences of my actions and become more aware of whether I am reactive or responsive in my decision making.

I had to create a set of what I now call "daily practices," which I could do for a minute, five minutes, or an hour every day. Daily practices are small changes that I make to my thinking and behaviors that allow me to create and sustain personal growth.

For my practices, I asked myself questions and then created the space and a process to help me answer these questions honestly. I had to ask myself questions such as "What is real, and what do I have to do to live my life as a more caring person?" I had not learned how to care for myself or be compassionate, so I did not like my initial answers because the answers really hurt. As I explored deeper, I realized that I was living a life that was hurtful and ego driven, and I had no one to blame except myself. It was mine to own.

I had to honestly look at all the hurt and pain I had caused others and myself through my behaviors.

On many challenging journeys, the first step can be the hardest. This was no different for me. I had to take the first difficult steps and honestly assess myself without excuses. I had to create daily practices, which I continue to use today, in order to propel myself forward and evolve my thinking and behaviors.

This book is about sharing stories and coming to the awareness that we all have a real-life experience that is a part of who we are and that dictates our behaviors. Throughout this book, I will share my experiences, and perhaps some of the stories I share may be a part of your story.

One of the goals of this book is to support you in creating daily practices that move you toward who you truly are and change how you want to be in your interactions. Each chapter will have a daily practice and process that you will be asked to do over and over for a period of time, perhaps your entire life. The processes in this book are designed to allow you to check in with each chapter, assess your daily practice, gauge your growth, and build your capacity. Invite an accountability partner to join you on the journey to practice and create accountability.

I had not learned how to care for myself or be compassionate, so I did not like my initial answers because the answers really hurt. As I explored deeper, I realized that I was living a life that was hurtful and ego driven, and I had no one to blame except myself. It was mine to own.

An accountability partner is someone whom you trust, whom you can read this book with, and with whom you can share the action steps you want to make. If he or she does not read this book with you, just ask him or her to check in with you and hold you accountable. The accountability partner's role is to check with you to see if you are on track with your commitments. The accountability partner is someone you will listen to and from whom you can take critical feedback in a way that supports your growth. By having an accountability partner, you are able to stay on track with your work of changing your thinking and behaviors as you move through the practices in this book. Building an accountability process and committing to an accountability partner should be one of your first steps.

> **Starting this journey of self-reflection was the hardest step because the truth was, I did not like my thoughts, my behavior, or myself.**
>
> **I had to create a set of practices that I could do for a minute, five minutes, or an hour every day.**

As I started my journey to self-awareness, I found that I could read all the greatest self-help books and go to all the latest self-help workshops, and at a certain point I still had to get down and do my own real work. What I have learned is that to promote and sustain change, we, as individuals, have to be willing to do our own daily work. For me, the biggest challenge was understanding what it meant to be doing "the work."

None of the workshops I attended nor the books I read provided me with a clear description of the steps I would need to take to do the "work" to truly become aware. Through the workshops and books, I received a clear message that my life was messed up and I had to do something about that, but there was never a clear process outlined to make these changes. I found that the first step was to be honest about where I currently was in my life. I had to accept myself for how I had been moving through my life, and I had to be brutally honest about the dysfunction in my thinking, behavior, and impact on others.

When I was not willing to be honest, it slowed my growth and awakening, and at a certain point, I decided that I had lived lies long enough. I fought being honest for years because I was operating from my ego perspective, which said that the world revolves around me and everyone else needs to change. Through my life, I had created a variety of narratives that drove my behavior. One of these

> **One of my first steps toward growth was to look within and examine my behavior to see myself as others saw me. I had to be willing to explore the stories that I told myself about who I was and why I behaved in the way I did.**

narratives said that I was the most important person, and if there was a problem, it was the other person's problem, because I was right and good. Another story was that I was a victim and the world owed me something for all the pain I had experienced.

The way that I treated people was not kind, and I had to first look within myself to understand what was driving this behavior. Playing a victim did not honestly help me see myself.

The work of personal change is manifested by creating and committing to practices that you can do throughout your day and week, to help you become more aware of your feelings, thoughts, and actions. Being conscious of committing to daily practice is key, because the goal is to grow your understanding of the consequences of your actions and whether you are reactive or responsive in your decision making. As I started doing daily practices, I noticed that a reactive step was based more on my judgmental story, and a responsive approach required me to think, process, and then make a decision outside of my ego.

Throughout the practices, I had to stay present to an awareness of judgment that leads to blame or shame; until I moved out of shaming and blaming myself, my life did not change. I had to have compassion and empathy for the parts that I disliked the most about myself to be able to move forward. We will talk more about what judgment that leads to blame or shame means in the section about personal agreements.

The first step cannot be missed or practiced lightly. Give yourself time to honestly assess yourself without excuses. The daily practices I use continue to propel me forward in evolving my thinking and behaviors. This evolution allows me to remain alert, responsive, and grateful for being present in my life.

This book is also about sharing our stories and coming to

As I started doing daily practices, I noticed that A REACTIVE STEP was based more on my judgmental story, and A RESPONSIVE APPROACH required me to think, process, and then make a decision outside of my ego.

the awareness that we all have a real-life experience that is a part of who we are. Throughout this book, I will share my experiences in my journey to engaging my self-awareness, and perhaps some of my stories may be a part of your story.

Some ways to use this book:

- ◆ Read each chapter and complete the daily reflective practice at the end of each chapter.

- ◆ If you are not ready to complete the daily reflective practice, read the chapter and come back to the daily practice when you are ready.

- ◆ Ideally, it is great to have someone to share the book processes so that you can hold each other accountable.

- ◆ If you do not have that person, join our online community to ask questions and provide feedback.

- ◆ Take your time and work through the book as you are comfortable.

The work of personal change is manifested by creating and committing to practices that you can do throughout your day and week, to help you become more aware of your feelings, thoughts, and actions.

We will start right away with your first daily reflective practice. The practices are designed to support you to make small changes that you can commit to over time, so you can grow continually and sustainably. The first daily practice is to conduct a self-assessment.

> **Until I moved out of shaming and blaming myself, my life did not change. I had to have compassion and empathy for the parts that I disliked the most about myself to be able to move forward.**

Chapter 1 Daily Reflective Practice
Self-Assessment

As an introduction to the work, it is beneficial to chart a course and start by conducting a personal self-assessment. Doing personal work is about being willing to go deep, learn to use self-reflection, and be brutally honest. I am going to share the process I used and share examples from my own personal self-assessment as a guide for this daily practice.

On a clean sheet of paper, draw lines to create four columns (see the Daily Reflective Practice #1 chart). The titles of the four columns should read My Thought, My Behavior, My Action, and Outcome.

Write down your daily common thoughts and their resulting behaviors and related outcomes. Do your best to leave your story out of it, and allow yourself to see your mindset and behavioral outcomes objectively. Conduct this daily practice with the objective of defining limiting behaviors that create outcomes that you do not like or that hurt others. Think about how you currently see and judge yourself. What are the self-protective strategies you use to protect yourself from seeing your thoughts, behaviors, and outcomes honestly?

Here is an example of my self-reflection list. This first process was the most challenging for me because I had to see my blind spots. I had to honestly look at how my behavior was affecting my relationships.

Daily Reflective Practice #1
Self-Assessment of My
Thoughts, Behaviors, and Actions

My Thought	My Behavior	My Action	Outcome
People make me mad.	Standoffish—Not willing to get to know others	Interactions that do not go well	Negative relationships
Judging other people	Do not allow people to get close; think the worst of them	Do not expose or open myself to others	No trust in others or myself to build relationships
I am a victim of other people's actions.	I behave as though other people can make me feel happy, sad, or other emotions through their actions.	I act sullen or disconnected until other people show me that they have my best interests at heart.	Disappointment because my expectations were not met and I continued distrust of people
I will never be successful.	I do not attempt to do anything that I am not familiar with or don't know how to do.	I say yes to things that I do not know about and do not always follow through to completion.	People lose faith in me, and I become resigned to the fact that I do not have what it takes to be successful in life.
The world revolves around me.	I do things that give me titles or perceived power.	I get involved in projects that elevate my ego by title or role.	I am never satisfied with where I am and I am constantly searching for more.

Read and reread your self-assessment list, and add to it as you see fit. Once you write something, don't go back and change it or cross it out because you have thought about it and changed your mind. Usually, the first thing you write is what is relevant, important, and affecting you the most.

You have to trust the process if you are going to make lasting change. This exercise may push you out of your comfort zone, and that is part of the process: to push you into your emotions, the feeling and learning zone. A challenge of personal work is to understand and be aware of the impact of your thoughts and behavior on life outcomes, not to continue to allow excuses to create a barrier to personal relationships and growth.

Take a moment to reflect on what it felt like to create your list of thoughts, behaviors, and outcomes, to see what they revealed about you. Were you able to look at yourself without judgment? Did you begin to defend or justify yourself? Did you do the writing exercise at all? We will revisit these daily practices in each subsequent chapter, and they will continue to build on each other.

Every chapter or sequence in the book will ask you to work on a daily reflective practice. It is an action step that you are encouraged to commit to every day until it becomes a part of your waking life. For each of you, that will be a different practice and time frame, depending on your level of work and commitment to transformation.

You have to trust the process
if you are going to make
lasting change.

Photo © Boris H. Pophristov

> "The Why of my personal work is important for me to understand because there has to be a compelling reason for me to persevere when I wanted to quit.

Photo © Boris H. Pophristov

The "Why"

The Why of my personal work is important to understand because there has to be a compelling reason for me to persevere when I wanted to quit. As a youth, I had no reason to persevere because of the hopeless victim story I told myself.

When I started thinking about becoming an empathetic and aware person, I had more questions than understanding. I found myself asking, why are empathy and compassion so important to me? Can I be in a place of empathy without knowing it? How does one act from an empathetic state of being? I had no connection to the answers and found my ego-based answers to be misleading. They were misleading because my thoughts and behaviors were filtered through my past experiences, which were loaded with judgments, blame, and shame. I also found that those judgmental thoughts were distractions from being present in my current experience, especially if those current experiences did not match my expectations.

So, I had to return to my heart and ask this question: Why do I want to do my own work, and what is this empathy I am pursuing? What I learned is that the big Why for me is that I want to make the world a more humane place. If I want a more humane world, then I have to become a more humane person. If I want to see people treat each other with more compassion and kindness, I need to feel and give that compassion and kindness. The importance of my Why drives me to stay in it when things get challenging and I want to blame, shame, or judge myself or other people.

> I had to return to my heart and ask this question: Why do I want to do my own work, and what is this empathy I am pursuing?

If you picked up this book, you are thinking about making a change in your life, and you are hoping that this will be the book that gets it done for you. If you read this book and never take action, you might as well put the book down now, because it will not do you any good. Personal change is not about which book or class will make you change. Personal change is about choosing to commit to taking action on a daily basis and doing something for yourself to change your thinking and behavior.

This book will do nothing for you until you choose to take action and create daily practices that reflect the changes you want to see in yourself. As you read this book, keep a journal, go deep into your thoughts without judgment that leads to blame or shame, and write your reflections on all of the daily practices before going on to the next chapter. Answer the questions honestly, take risks in making personal changes, and work with someone you trust who will hold you accountable.

If you picked up this book, you are thinking about making a change in your life, and you are hoping that this will be the book that gets it done for you.

Meet with other people who are reading this book, and have conversations with them about what you are feeling and processing through reading this book and committing to the daily practices. Ask a friend or family member to read it with you. Many people stop doing the work because they say the practice is redundant or tiring, and it certainly can be. Commit to practicing a new thought or behavior every day. Make incremental changes. You may have to go back and reread sections or adapt an earlier daily practice. Transformational change comes from making a commitment to fully embrace your own work. Don't let anything keep you from your stated objectives.

One of my greatest lessons in the dance of personal growth is that the personal work is about "practice and not perfection." I will never be a perfect person, and "perfect" is contextual, judgmental, and based on each person's lived experience. Once I rid myself of the expectation that I have to be "perfect," I can more effectively engage in my practice on a daily basis.

Awareness without action gets you nowhere, so throughout this book think about the daily practices you will use to heighten your awareness. Take each reflective practice seriously, and make sure you are clear as you move into each subsequent chapter and reflective practice. Taking consistent and intentional action is the only way that you will make the sustainable changes you want in yourself.

Examples of my Why and personal goals:

- ◆ The Why for me is to make the world a more humane place, and I have to start with myself.

- ◆ The Why for me is to learn to live in the present moment and be more aware of my biases in relationships.

- ◆ The Why for me is to learn to be empathetic toward others and understand that everyone has a valid life experience that may differ from mine.

Some of my goals for my personal work:

- ◆ Create a deeper understanding of who I am and how my past experiences affect my current day-to-day interactions.

- ◆ Build an understanding of my cultural and ethnic background.

- Design an internal process to support growth in awareness and actively make changes.

- Understand how to infuse self-awareness and understanding to build empathy while supporting and maintaining my changes.

Chapter 1 Daily Reflective Practice
What Is Your Why? What Are Your Goals?

Take some time to define why you want to read this book and do your own personal work. What do you want to change in your thinking and behaviors? How deep is your commitment? Why do you want to be more aware, and what actions do you want to take? What are the goals you want to achieve as you design your change process? Are you going to hold yourself accountable or ask someone else to? What is currently happening in your life that you are not satisfied with? What parts of yourself are you covering and not fully experiencing?

Take some real time to sit and ask your heart these questions.

Do not rush this process. When you are ready, take out your journal and start to write your Why. Write down why you want to grow personally, and be specific about who or what you might be in this new version of yourself.

Use a brainstorming practice to begin the process. A brainstorming process is where you write down everything you are thinking related to your Why and goals without judgment or defense. When you are brainstorming, all thoughts are valid, and there is no need to defend them or eliminate them because your mind says they are not possible. Criticism is not used, and the quantity of ideas is important to the process. Brainstorming allows you to think big crazy ideas, and sometimes the craziest thought or idea is the one that gets you most excited.

Write down these questions in your journal:

- ♦ Why do I want to grow? What is my Why?

- ♦ What behaviors do I want to change?

- ♦ What emotion do I want to feel or change?

- ♦ Add any other questions you feel will help you move through this brainstorming process.

Let words or phrases come into your awareness, and write the words or phrases without any evaluation or judgment. When you are tempted to overthink or second guess yourself by saying something like, "I am not sure how I want to say that," let that thought go. In brainstorming, you are writing thoughts based on what is at the top of your mind as you think about why you want to do this personal work. No defense, no justification or judgment.

Give yourself a fair amount of time to start this process, and take breaks when you need to. Reflection happens over time; you need to give yourself time for your process to unfold.

Once you have brainstormed some words and phrases, see if you can shorten it to a sentence or two. Talk about your Why with your accountability partner and see what he or she thinks.

When you are brainstorming, all thoughts are valid, and there is no need to defend them or eliminate them because your mind says they are not possible.

"

Being biased is part of the human experience. When we view bias through the lens of negativity and as someone who is bigoted, discriminatory, and hurtful, we remove our ability to talk about how our biases affect our relationships.

Photo © Boris H. Pophristov

"

"Circumstances do not make the man, they reveal him."

—James Allen

Chapter 2

Choosing to Become Aware

Before you read this chapter, take out your Why and the Self-Assessment worksheet where you listed your thoughts and behaviors.

♦ How did it feel to go through the process of assessing yourself?

♦ What types of changes do you want to make to more closely align with your Why?

♦ How did you feel, emotionally, as you went through the first two daily practices?

♦ If you were asked to share your Why, could you, and would it be consistent every time you shared your Why?

Talk with your accountability partner and share your challenges and growth with the self-assessment and Why daily practice. Once you have completed that conversation, dive into the next chapter.

> **Self-awareness is about living and being in the moment and relating to your personal interactions from a realistic perspective.**

I want to share a few things to think about as you dive into your work of developing self-awareness. Self-awareness is about living and being in the moment and relating to your personal interactions from a realistic perspective. As you embark on this process, think about this question: "Does my lack of self-awareness inhibit or enhance my ability to be in an authentic relationship?" That question asks you to explore whether you are getting to know the person in front of you based on your authentic interaction with him or her or based on the story you have about that person through your biased judgments.

When I was unaware, the story I made up about a person and my interaction with him or her was based on my judgments connected to a past experience I had had with someone who somehow resembled that person or experience in front of me. Something about the other person got me emotionally charged when I interacted with him or her because I was unconscious. If I am really honest, at the time I did not even care why I did not like the person.

As an unaware person, I did not know how to think or talk about what I was experiencing through my own judgments. I had no idea how to communicate what I was feeling to the other person. I knew only that the other person was wrong and all I had to do was convince him or her.

> **As an unaware person, I did not know how to think or talk about what I was experiencing through my own judgments.**

My communication skills were designed to control and manipulate other people, and I did not realize how much my judgmental and controlling behavior was stunting my growth.

To help you understand why communication work is so important, I want to share a couple of perspectives on how we currently have conversations about challenging topics such as judgment, race, class, and bias. Let's start with race conversations. Think about when you have experienced any conversations about race and the conversations digressed into people being told or feeling like they have been called a racist. What happens to the conversation? Typically, the person who gets called the racist gets defensive and shuts down, and the ability to build a relationship is minimized. Once people have an experience where they feel like they have been called a racist or any other label related to race, class, gender, sexual orientation, religion, etc., the conversation shuts down, and the relationship is negatively affected.

The conversation shuts down because the accusers try to justify why they are right, and the accused defend why they are not that label: racist, sexist, homophobic, anti-Semitic, etc. The accusers justify, and the accused defend themselves. This is a lose-lose conversation because whenever we go to a defend/justify conversation, someone is always going to lose, and the relationship suffers.

> **Something about the other person got me emotionally charged when I interacted with him or her because I was unconscious.**

There is a similar phenomenon that happens around the word *biased*. Take a moment and think about this. If I were to introduce myself to you by saying, "Good day, my name is Bill, and I am biased," where are the first places your mind goes? Talk with your accountability buddy and ask him or her what he or she thinks about someone who is biased. If you are like most people, your mind typically goes to something negative, and you assume a biased person is bigoted, discriminatory, hateful, or hurtful. So we do not talk about race because we do not want to be accused of being racist, and we don't talk about biases because we, as a society, have attached a negative connotation to the word *biased*.

As a noun, *bias* is defined as a particular tendency, trend, inclination, feeling, or opinion, especially one that is preconceived or unreasoned. The definition does not say bias is good or bad; it says a bias is created from an experience I have had that I add judgment and meaning to. The reason I am biased is that my thoughts, feelings, and actions are filtered through my own experience, and I am prejudging new people based on my past interactions with similar people.

What I know today is that being biased is part of the human experience. When we view bias through the lens of negativity and as someone who is bigoted, discriminatory, and hurtful, we essentially remove our ability to talk about how our biases affect our relationships.

What I know today is that being biased is part of the human experience.

If we cannot talk about the impacts of race and bias because of fear, we will never disrupt the status quo.

What we have done is taken a characteristic that describes every living, breathing human being on the planet and created such a negative definition and feeling that we don't talk about the impacts of our biases in our interactions with each other. If we cannot talk about the impacts of race and bias because of fear, we will never disrupt the status quo. Is it possible to normalize conversations on bias, and really own and understand the impacts our personal biases have in our relationships? I believe it is possible to normalize conversations on bias if we are willing to do our own personal work.

> **I believe that there is a process to understanding the impacts of our biases and also to understanding that every bias has an origination point.**

What I learned about myself is that I judged and treated people based on what I had seen, heard, or experienced with members of their groups in the past, and I was completely unaware that that was what I was doing. I reacted to new people from those groups without having the factual truth about who they were because I was biased toward them from a past experience.

I believe that there is a process to understanding the impacts of our biases and also to understanding that every bias has an origination point. The origination point is the place where the original experience happened that created the biased judgment. The origination point is the point of healing, compassion, and understanding. An objective for me in "doing my work" is to get to the origination point of my biased experiences because understanding the origination point is an important step in forgiving others and ourselves.

To achieve a greater state of awareness, we also have to be

honest and willing to see our inner biases toward those parts of ourselves that we have labeled bad, ugly, unworthy, etc. I had plenty of words that I used to describe myself, and when I started this process, most of my self-descriptors were ugly. What is the negative word or words that you use to describe the side of yourself that you despise or judge as ugly or not good enough? To do this work, you have to be honest and willing to be open to other possibilities.

The origination point is the place where the original experience happened that created the biased judgment. The origination point is the point of healing, compassion, and understanding.

To become aware of the impacts of our biases when in relationships, we need to be critically honest. Steps in bias awareness are the following:

- ◆ Be open to examining our perception of ourselves
- ◆ To understand the evolution of personal bias, so that we can heal with compassion and empathy
- ◆ To become aware of the emotional and behavioral impacts of bias when in relationships
- ◆ To see ourselves with unflinching clarity, which leads us to more freedom and integrity

Self-examination requires you to engage in this growth and healing process while being aware of self-judgment that leads to self-blame and self-shame. By making a working agreement to see your inner critic without letting it run the show, you can move into your work in a way that will support sustainable growth. Personal agreements allow you to create a format of accountability that will carry you through the processes you are using for your daily practices. The following personal agreement daily practice will support you in creating your own set of personal agreements.

Chapter 2 Daily Reflective Practice
Personal Agreements

This daily practice is designed to deepen your self-awareness and help you create habits that support your personal work. Remember that the work is not only about reading this book; the work is being willing to explore yourself and do what you need to grow.

To be successful, the first step to bring to your work is a willingness to honestly assess yourself and how you interact with others you are in a relationship with. You practiced this with your self-assessment at the beginning of this book and then reflected on your Why.

To take this a step further, talk with someone who knows you and cares about your growth to get critical feedback. The feedback you are asking for is about your growth areas. Having this conversation enables you to deepen your exploration of your thoughts, behaviors, outcomes, and actions. In combination, the verbal and written processes are designed to deepen your learning when combined with the daily practices.

> **By making a working agreement to see your inner critic without letting it run the show, you can move into your work in a way that will support sustainable growth.**

It was, and still is, really hard to hear people tell me about my growth areas, but over time, the conversation has enabled me to face my growth areas, begin to accept them, and, if needed, apologize for any hurt I caused. This approach in looking at myself is wrapped around a mirror metaphor. The mirror relates to looking inside when something happens in your life first, and this can grow more self-reflection practices. Using self-reflection, I learned to make a commitment to eliminating the behaviors that lead to my negative outcomes. I have learned that I can only do my best, each day, moving forward. I am not perfect, and I cannot go back and heal all the negative consequences of my behavior. I can only forgive, learn, and move forward.

Read this book with a friend, so you can support each other's conversation and hold each other accountable. Margaret Wheatley said, "When we begin listening to each other, and when we talk about things that matter to us, the world begins to change." This work has the potential to change you and your world.

Let's take another step to build the system that will support your change. To begin creating your support system, you have to create some personal agreements.

Personal Agreements

Personal agreements are designed to build a foundation for behavioral expectations about how to treat yourself throughout your process of change. Personal agreements are essentially the agreements you make with yourself to stay committed to your path and hold yourself accountable for the actions that you choose to take. In every group I have facilitated over the last 10 years, I have had the participants create personal agreements because the agreements really support highly functioning and deep conversations.

> **Your personal agreements are the agreements you make with yourself to stay committed to your path and hold yourself accountable for the actions that you choose to take.**

Here are some of the agreements

I use that have supported others and me in making lasting changes:

◆ Awareness of judgment that leads to blame or shame. This agreement is not about attempting to stop judging, because that would be impossible. We are always judging, discerning, and thinking about the interactions we are having, consciously or unconsciously. The idea behind this agreement is to heighten your level of self-awareness so you know when you have just dropped into judgment. When I drop into judgment in an interaction, I drop out of being present, because judgments live in the stories I've told myself in my head. I am judging my interaction with you based on the story I am telling myself about you in my head, which typically has nothing to do with the realities of our interaction. The change action is to heighten self-awareness to the point that you are able to be aware that you dropped into judgment and push yourself out of judgment to be present. The judgment will only affect the relationship when it comes out of your mouth, and the change is to gain control of what comes out of your mouth.

> **When I drop into judgment in an interaction, I drop out of being present, because judgments live in the stories I've told myself in my head.**

- You can also add self to this personal agreement: awareness of self-judgment that leads to self-blame or self-shame.

- Set aside all electronics—phones, tablets, computers, etc. Eliminating the electronic distractions when doing your work will allow you to remain present. You can send that text later.

- Be kind to yourself.

- Allow for processing time. You don't have to get it all at once. Take the time to digest what you are reading and journaling. Do not rush your process.

- Take breaks. Breathe. Take care of your body when it starts to get stressed.

Think about other personal agreements that are going to be important for you as you dive deeper into self-reflection and change. You will be challenged and emotional at times throughout this process, so having agreements with yourself is essential to sustain change.

This is another reason why having a reading and accountability partner is helpful, because you can keep each other on task. Having someone who cares about you, to hold you accountable, will support you when you get off track. When you ask someone to be your accountability partner, explain to him or her specifically what you want him or her to do. For example, I asked my accountability partner to talk to me when I don't follow through with a project or behavior I have committed to change. Decide what you want from your accountability partner and have conversations with him or her as you move forward.

Build Your Personal Agreements

Use some of the personal agreements listed here, add to them to make them your own, and create your own personal agreements about how you will treat yourself while working through these processes. Think about what it will take for you to be honest, reflective, and realistic with this work. What agreements do you need to make with yourself to be fully engaged and not give up when things get challenging? How will you hold yourself accountable to infusing your personal agreements into daily practices?

Once you are satisfied, write them down and put them in places where you can see them daily. Use the list as a living document, and when you think another personal agreement is needed, add it to the list. I have worked with groups that set up personal agreements, and after breaks, I noticed people were coming in late so I asked to add another agreement and we agreed to add honor time. Use these agreements to set the culture and accountability structure for your learning.

> **Having someone who cares about you, to hold you accountable, will support you when you get off track.**

> I will never be perfect, and even the word *perfect* is based on each person's perspective, so there is no need to strive for perfection.

"

"Be not afraid of growing slowly,
be afraid only of standing still."

—Chinese Proverb

Chapter 3

First Steps

Let's start with a quick check-in. Have you finished creating your personal thought/behavior reflection? Have you discovered your Why? Have you created your personal agreements? If you have not completed these tasks, please go back and do so or keep reading and complete the steps when you are ready.

I am writing this as a man in my 60s, reflecting on the lessons that eluded me as a young man. If I am honest with myself, I did not see these lessons or start living consciously until my mid-40s, and I am a constant work in progress; every day is a challenge to stay self-aware and present. Today, I realize the importance of being aware of my thoughts, behaviors, and actions, because I have deeply felt the negative impacts of my unconscious behavior on others and myself for much of my life.

The work for me was, and is, to be self-aware and to connect that awareness to how I think about and interact with people. Through awareness, I can create new thoughts and behaviors that are more authentic and honor myself and the other person. My mindset that supports me in moving forward is that my work in this life is about "practice and not perfection." I will never be perfect, and even the word *perfect* is based on each person's perspective, so there is no need to strive for perfection.

> If I am honest with myself, I did not see these lessons or start living consciously until my mid-40s, and I am a constant work in progress; every day is a challenge to stay self-aware and present.

From my current perspective of understanding and awareness, I will share with you what I believe was happening to me as I went through a transformation starting at 17 years old. Through this book, I will be telling stories of how I lived as a young person who was unconscious and the steps I took to start this journey. I will start by sharing my first step, which was the hardest.

Remember that I was completely unaware that the following

things were happening as a 13-year-old, 18-year-old, 30-year-old … and I am able to understand it now only after years of self-reflection and doing my own work.

> **My mindset that supports me in moving forward is that my work in this life is about "practice and not perfection."**

The first thing I did was to get myself to a place where I could not stand my life. To move out of being a victim, I had to take responsibility for allowing my behavior to persist. I had to own that I had made decisions that were hurtful to others and myself. I also had to acknowledge that I generally did not care about how the other person felt, and I rationalized that the people around me deserved the treatment I was giving them because I was a victim and they were bad, while I was a victim of my circumstances. It got to the point where I hated myself for doing what I did to others, and yet I did not know what to do to turn things around. I knew that I was not happy, had no friends, hurt people, and was in trouble a lot.

I had to look deeply within myself to understand the way and the why within my interactions before I could accept how bad I was at the time. The first step was the hardest, because I was angry and that anger had so much negative emotion attached to it that it scared me. I had to get to the origination point of my emotional hatred and start to change my negative outlook about myself, and that was not going to be easy. For me, the origination point was very scary.

All of my biases are connected by an emotion-filled origination point. The origination point is the place where the initial interaction that created the bias occurred. The biased interaction happened with a person or people, and the interaction may not have gone well, and I attributed the behavior of one or a few to the entire group. Along with the experience, there is also a narrative or story that went along with the experience. Every bias has both an experiential action and a narrative or story that reinforces the bias over time. The origination point is important to understand because this is the point of awareness and healing. Many of the biases I describe as an adult were created between birth and adolescence and continuously are reflected in my interactions.

> **I had to look deeply within myself to understand the way and the why within my interactions before I could accept how bad I was at the time.**

What I have learned is that many of my current emotionally charged interactions that support my biases are rooted in the past and get confirmed in my present interactions. There are two types of biases: implicit and explicit. As diverse as we are, all human beings are alike in that we all have biases, both known and unknown to us. Biases are age based, gender based, geographically based, religious, and political, and no one escapes his or her biases.

Implicit biases are the biases that are unconscious; we are not aware of them. Explicit biases are the ones we are aware of, though we may be unconscious of their impact. If we are unaware (implicit bias), these biases act themselves out as language and behaviors that cause relationships to disintegrate without giving us any understanding of what or why they happened.

> **The first step was the hardest, because I was angry and that anger had so much negative emotion attached to it that it scared me.**

As a young adolescent, I had an unknown (implicit) bias against men from my interactions with my dad, who was verbally and physically demeaning to me when I was very young. As an adolescent, I was not aware of the bias, and it showed up in me not trusting "men," whether they were my brother, a teacher, or the man who lived next door. The bias was implicit because I was not aware that it was happening at the time. From the bias I had against men, I did not trust men, and I knew that they would be nice to me for only a certain amount of time. From that unconsciously biased lens, I usually destroyed the relationship before those men could destroy me; at least, that is the story I told myself. The unconscious bias caused me to treat men the way I learned from my experiences with my dad.

When I am aware of my bias (explicit bias), I know and understand the impact of my behavior. I know (explicit) that I have a bias against bad drivers. I was a very bad driver as a teenager and created this bias against bad drivers through that experience. The origination point of both of these biases happened between my birth and adolescence. Most of the biases we have are experienced or given to us between birth and adolescence, and we manifest the truth of the bias through our adult life. I manifested my bias against men by interacting with a man and having my negative behavior and words go terribly wrong. I would then blame that man and walk away saying, "I was right. All men are jerks."

> **Typically, from the state of explicit bias, I did not care about those I hurt, because I was unaware and I had labeled them as unlikable and wrong.**

Typically, from the state of explicit bias, I did not care about those I hurt, because I was unaware and I had labeled them as unlikable and wrong. I knew that was how they were because that was the behavioral pattern I connected to the bias about them. I was prone to blame the interaction on the other person and promote a victim mentality for myself. I used my victim perspective as a reason to justify my behavior. "I have been hurt by that group, so why not hurt them back and then blame them for it?"

We all have a story about where we are and who we are in life. The story is based upon a view of the world that we think is right, and that experience is what we label as real. Once I label my experience, it lets loose a complete set of behaviors, thoughts, and actions that then dictate my reactions to the person. As a victim, I would blame these reactions on the other person.

I now look at these as my biased behaviors, and I often wonder what it would be like if I were to go through my life experiences with fewer biased behaviors that label, control, and direct my actions. How could I change my reactions to have a more thoughtful response to that person in my life? How could I act with less judgment, shame, or blame? Is it even possible to live life in the moment without thinking about what is coming next? Is it the thought or the emotions behind the thought that have scared me? These are the questions I had to start asking, and these questions continue to guide my journey and push me to continue my own work.

The perspective on bias that I use is the following:

- ◆ Bias is simply each person's unique predisposition to seeing the world. It's our own prejudice in thinking when we are confronted with new events.
- ◆ Bias is used to describe a tendency or preference toward a particular perspective, ideology, or result.
- ◆ Biases come with a prescribed set of language, behaviors, and actions.

- All information and points of view generate some form of bias.

There is a lot of research on implicit and explicit bias awareness that you can explore. People who are biased toward others believe that the behavior they are using is deserved without any awareness of or care for the impact on the other person. In an unconsciously biased experience, there is no connection to reality or truth. The interaction is based on the story I have in my head.

The various types of biases show up as prejudices, stereotyping, and discrimination. Biases are extrapolated onto a group based on the experience with a few and in some cases one person. My dad was one man, and from my interactions with him, I created a bias that all men are mean. I extrapolated the experience of one person to an entire group and treated men from my

All information and points of view generate some form of bias.

discriminatory and biased perspective. I had no idea this was happening and knew only that my interactions with men always went poorly.

I learned that my biased interactions started with me getting emotionally charged and then making judgments about the other person based on a past experience with people like him or her. I judged people based on what I had seen, heard, or experienced about members of their groups in the past, and I was completely unaware I was doing that. Judgments and assumptions are a precursor to biases, and becoming aware of my own judgments was a step in my growth. When I knew I was judging, I was able to calm myself more quickly because I could use my judgment as a warning signal that a biased behavior was coming up.

My practice was that over time I was able to become more aware of my own trigger points and own them. The sooner I became aware of my trigger points, the more aware I became of my judgments. I could then learn to better control my actions and limit my unconscious reactions.

The stories I wove into my life experiences and behaviors unconsciously directed my decision making each day. The story in my head about who I was in this life was a mix of fact and fantasy. It reminds me of a Gil Scott-Heron song I loved and listened to called "A Legend in His Own Mind." I truly was a legend in my own mind. I did not understand why other people did not interact with me in a way that reflected how important I thought I was. For the first half of my life, I did not know what a real and authentic personal interaction experience was or felt like.

I started to wonder how present and connected I was to each moment and each interaction. Was I being factual or making up a legend story in my head?

Through my biases and judgments, I kept bumping into myself and getting in the way of my real experiences in the moment. There were times when I had to make up a fanciful story because I was so hurt and hurtful toward others that the legend story was easier. I justified my behavior because my life was filled with a lot of pain and grief at a young age.

One of the hardest steps for me was to look at my judgment and my explosive, emotional anger and to own the negative impacts my thoughts and behaviors had on other people.

Chapter 3 Daily Reflective Practice
Judgment and Bias Awareness

The daily practice for this chapter is to think about your most recent interactions where you got emotionally charged, angry, or judgmental toward another person.

- ◆ What was the judgment and bias you had about that person?

- ◆ Was this person a member of your family, a professional colleague, or someone in your daily experience? Does it matter who the person you are judging is?

- What was the story you told yourself about that person?
- Think about the story you told yourself about the interaction, and whether you blamed the other person or felt like you were the victim.
- Think about your own personal biases and how you used them in that emotionally charged interaction.
- What was the personal experience that created your judgment?

Write in your journal the answers to these questions, and have a conversation with your accountability partner about an emotionally charged experience you had and the judgments you made. Be honest about your role in the interaction and be specific about the behaviors you used. Being specific and honest about the behaviors allows you to think about the origination point of the biased experience and the narrative associated with the bias.

Take some time to process this practice as you deepen your awareness of your own behaviors.

I learned that my biased interactions started with me getting emotionally charged and then making judgments about the other person based on a past experience with people like him or her.

> That healing process allowed me to be more conscious of how my past experiences affected my present interactions.

Photo © Will Dickey

"

"The secret of getting ahead is getting started."

—Mark Twain

Chapter 4

The Origination Point

Reflect on the daily practices you have created up to this point, and think about the progress you are making. How are you doing with your:

- ♦ Self-assessment?
- ♦ Why?
- ♦ Personal agreements?
- ♦ Judgment and bias awareness?

Have you continued the practices? What are some of the results you are seeing? How is the relationship with your accountability partner? Are you honest and open to your reflections? What is your emotional state of being? What will you celebrate about the mindset shifts and behavioral changes you have accomplished?

The origination point is one of the most important discoveries in this journey. Once I understood the importance of the origination point of biases, there was a healing process that started. That healing process allowed me to be more conscious of how my past experiences affected my present interactions. I became more aware of the starting point of what I was thinking about other people and was learning to be more authentic.

> **I was dying inside, I was hurting other people, and I had to find the origination point of my judgments and biases because my biases and judgments were controlling all of my interactions.**

Origination is defined as the process of bringing something into existence. In bias awareness, the origination point is the place in life where the experience that created a bias occurred. There is an origination point for all biases that we experience as human beings, and no one can escape that; we can choose only to be unconscious.

When I shared the story about my dad's behavior toward me, I said that as an adolescent I created a bias that all men are mean. The way my bias showed up as an adolescent and into my adult life was based on how I interpreted the men in my present day in relation to the original experience. I could not fully heal the explosive emotional impact of my biases solely on how I experienced the bias as an adult. To fully understand and heal myself, I had to get to the origination point. The origination point of my bias with my dad was as a young person between the ages of 8 and 12.

Once I understood the importance of the origination point of biases, there was a healing process that started. That healing process allowed me to be more conscious of how my past experiences affected my present interactions.

When I was deep into my work in my mid-20s, to heal the bias that all men are mean meant that I had to get to the origination point. The origination point of my biased experiences became the point of understanding and healing.

As you read this chapter, think about the origination point of the biases and judgments you shared in the previous chapter.

To make the changes I have made in my life today, I had to look at the many parts of myself that I experienced as normal behavior, because I was not aware of how abhorrent, abnormal, and hurtful my behavior was to other people. I had to reflect on the real impact of my behavior on people. I realized that the behavior I normalized and used was taught to me growing up or learned as a survival strategy, and I had become numb to the impacts I had on other people.

I was dying inside, I was hurting other people, and I had to find the origination point of my judgments and biases because my biases and judgments were controlling all of my interactions. As I started to become aware, I started thinking about the hurt I had done in my life, and it was eating me up inside because I knew that hurt was the experience that many people had with me.

> **The scared feelings and fears that I carried were based on real interactions with my dad, and they caused me to build up a lot of anger and hate in my heart.**

As a teenager, I knew I was mean and mad. Those mean and mad emotions and thoughts were my first model at home, and that is what I replicated in my relationships with others and myself. Sometimes I caught myself treating family, friends, and my own children with the same anger. I realized, after years of my own work, that I was scared a lot as a young person because I grew up in an environment never knowing which of my behaviors would set off the anger in my dad.

The scared feelings and fears that I

carried were based on real interactions with my dad, and they caused me to build up a lot of anger and hate in my heart. I also understand today that I took that anger, hate, and fear into school, relationships, and everything I did growing up. As a young person, I saw violent behavior toward myself and other family members. That visual violence created expectations and behaviors that were reinforced through my parents' negative modeling of relationship. I took those behaviors and integrated them into my relationship with everyone, including my children.

As a parent, I saw that my children replicated everything I did, and they mirrored my behavior back to me. That was not always easy to see because many times the reflection I saw in my children was my negative behavior. For those of you who are parents, I would ask you to think about the following questions: "What past unconscious behaviors, thoughts, and actions are replicating themselves in your current reality as a parent? How are those past experiences reflected to you through the lens of your children?" Some of my greatest lessons were learned through observing my children, and I had to work hard to change my life with my own children. I did not want to replicate the home life I was raised with, for myself, my partner, and my children.

A day in my young life was living in a chaotic, disconnected environment where there was little to no real communication. I had four siblings: two older sisters, an older brother, and a younger sister. My oldest sister, Judy, was 10 years older than me. By the time I was 8, she had left the house, and she passed away in 2015. My next sister, Lee, was my protector, and she helped me more than I understood while she was alive. Lee died suddenly when I was 13 in 1969, and my life was never the same after that. My brother, Rich, and I had a challenging relationship growing up, and we have had to work to establish a loving and authentic connection. My youngest sister, Kathy, just got left behind, so I did not really get to know her until we connected later in our adult life. The home life was so crazy that all of us kids wanted only to turn 18 and leave home.

Family relationships were controlling, demanding, and demeaning, and I learned that the way I should behave in a relationship is to try to control the other person. My dad had two different personalities when he came home. One personality was kind of nice and engaged, and the other one was sheer anger: openly venting toward my mom, my sister Lee, and me. I felt like a top being flipped over and over, one moment receiving "I love you," and the next receiving blazing rage for the most childish behavior. I was hit in punishment for childhood explorations such as taking the cover of the lawn sprinkler off. The sprinkler

> **Family relationships were controlling, demanding, and demeaning, and I learned that the way I should behave in a relationship is to try to control the other person.**

at our house was on, and I was outside playing alone when I unscrewed the cap. Water was going everywhere, and I ran into the house soaking wet. My dad got angry and scolded me as if I had done something terrible. Then we went to the garage, where I was expected to bend over, grab my ankles, and wait for him to hit me, usually with a wooden paddle that had "board of education" printed on it.

The only reason the title "board of education" is significant is that when I was in my 40s, I served on a school board of education and was the president of the board for two years. In my teens, it sucked to get hit with the board of education paddle, and these days it is both funny and ironic. Back to my sprinkler story.

> **The story I told myself was that I could not be curious and explore or I would get hit.**

As a parent today, the fix for me would be to turn the sprinkler off, grab a towel, and have a good laugh with my kid. The reason that story is so important to me is that telling the story allows me to acknowledge the past and understand how those connections affected my interactions.

The story I told myself was that I could not be curious and explore or I would get hit. My dad did not explicitly say that I could not explore or be curious. My head made up that story, and so I did not look to do things outside of my comfort zone. Whether I made up the story or someone directly told me not to explore or be curious, my story became the truth.

I believe that curiosity and exploration are childhood experiences that allow for adult growth. Those negative interactions with my dad took away my curiosity, my willingness to do different things, and my ability to explore as a child and adult. As a child, I got in trouble for exploring and being creative, so I stopped doing both as a child, an adolescent, and an adult.

Everyone has a story, and there are reasons why we behave the way we do. It took me a long time to be able to acknowledge my story with as little judgment, shame, or blame as possible. The more honest I was about my story, the more clarity came to me.

The beatings began at 9 years old, and they came along with the narrative, from my dad, that I would never amount to anything. The messages were delivered through many different channels: verbal abuse, being hit with a wooden paddle, being left waiting in the driveway for hours to be picked up. I had anger, disappointment, and a lack of a true connection with my parents in my youth. I am not sure if my mom understood the depth of what was

> **Everyone has a story, and there are reasons why we behave the way we do. … The more honest I was about my story, the more clarity came to me.**

happening to our family because she was treated in the same way by my dad. There were many harmful parts of the story for me as I observed physical abuse and damaging and demeaning comments toward family members. Many days, I heard my dad's voice in my head saying, "You are a failure who will never amount to anything."

The message of being a failure was the story I carried around in my head for much of my adolescence and into adulthood. Even if I was successful at something, this narrative of being a failure was driving my relationships, interactions, and behaviors. The bulk of all this was happening between ages 9 and 16, and I developed into the mean kid who was not willing to explore myself or anything outside of myself because I was a triggered victim.

> **The narrative of being a failure haunted me for years because I was unconscious of how my behavior, words, and emotions hurt other people.**

The narrative of being a failure haunted me for years because I was unconscious of how my behavior, words, and emotions hurt other people. I was not even aware that this hurtful language and behavior was happening. Eventually, I learned that the story of my upbringing and the language that was used were meaningful and had major impacts on my personality and the way I interacted in my relationships.

I carried the failure story for a long time, and I knew that no matter what I did, I would never be good enough. I unconsciously told myself I could not and would not be successful in school, work, and pretty much all of the relationships I had. Most of the relationships I had, for much of my life, reflected in some way the relationships I experienced at home. The experiences with my dad hurt me deeply, and I know that I unknowingly took that hurt and gave it to others in my own relationships. The hurt feelings really bothered me, and it seemed to me that my dad wanted me to have a hurt reaction for some level of parental satisfaction. The story I told myself was that my dad did those things to me because he hated me and he got some kind of twisted pleasure from seeing me hurt. I had so much emotional pain as a child that, as an adolescent, I did not want to feel. When I was 13, I did not want him to know how much he hurt me, so I made a decision not to show him my emotions. I had been beaten and hurt for so long that I remember one day when I was grabbing my ankles telling myself that I would never let him see me cry again.

> **The experiences with my dad hurt me deeply, and I know that I unknowingly took that hurt and gave it to others in my own relationships.**

I thought I was so smart to shut off my tears and sadness and not give him the satisfaction of seeing me in pain. What I realized, as I started doing my own personal work, is that by shutting off my emotions of hurt and sadness to spite him, I was shutting off all of my emotions. The decision that day to shut down emotionally affected me for years because shutting down my emotions of hurt and sadness prevented any chance of learning from and experiencing any of my emotions.

> **The day I shut down my hurt and sadness emotions, I stopped any chance of learning and experiencing all emotions.**

Compassion, care, and empathy were shut down that day, as well. I had no idea how that one decision would affect the rest of my life. Along the way, I ended up hurting myself and others in ways I never could have imagined.

In my attempt to avoid the pain of those beatings, I never understood that I would be relinquishing my connection to joy, love, or happiness. I later learned that all feelings are stored in the same place in the body. As a teenager, I could not have guessed that shutting off my hurt and pain meant that I was shutting down my access to every other emotion. By endeavoring to deny the pain, I destroyed my access to empathy, compassion, and care. This is another one of those experiences and life decisions that followed me for years, infiltrating all of my interactions, while creating personal and relational behaviors that matched my hurt.

At 13 years old, I had an experience that scared me and

showed me how volatile and angry I was. I was helping my dad work on cars because that was what he thought I needed to learn. It was fun to learn about cars, and I did not mind learning with him at first. Over time, the car repairs got more complicated, and that required special tools that I had not learned about. During the car work, my dad would often yell at me if I didn't understand him or took too long to find a tool, and I was too scared to even say that I could not find it.

Over time, my dad wiped out my enjoyment of working on cars with him by how he treated me. After a couple of years of that demeaning treatment, I snapped. I still get emotionally charged when I reflect on this experience because it goes deep and it affected me on many levels.

As we worked that day, his behavior became more verbally demeaning and physically abusive. When I could not find a tool fast enough, he would yell, call me names, and push my head into the toolbox. On this particular day, I looked hard into the toolbox and just did not know what the tool he was asking for even looked like. I could feel him coming up behind me, and as he came up behind me, I felt him grab my head. This time, he stuffed

> **The experiences with my dad hurt me deeply, and I know that I unknowingly took that hurt and gave it to others in my own relationships.**

my face into the toolbox to help me find it. It really hurt. After a minute or so, I pulled up, looked at him with hate burning in my eyes, and told him, "If you ever touch me again, I will kill you." He looked at me and stepped away, and I ran out of the garage. At that moment, I knew I could kill him and probably not care, and this was one of the scariest turning points in my angry life.

Thinking about that today scares me because I realize that as an adolescent and young adult I had no compassion or empathy for other people and I justified myself by saying I was a child of abuse and divorce. My life was completely driven by my hurt ego, with little care for the feelings of others. It was not until into my late 20s and early 30s that I started to understand what was happening to me. The daily experience of my house growing up was one of danger, insecurity, and confusion, and I took those behaviors into all my interactions. When it came time to do my own work, I learned that I had to get to the origination point of my pain in order to heal and move forward.

After a minute or so, I pulled up, looked at him with hate burning in my eyes, and told him, "If you ever touch me again, I will kill you."

Getting to the origination point of my bias (that all men are mean) in my 20s meant that I had to go back to the 9-year-old boy and start a healing process. All of the emotion and hurt that I carried from my childhood had to be accepted and faced before I could start to move forward. The process was really challenging because I had to feel and resurface all the anger and emotion that I had shut down as a child and adolescent. I had to accept that I was hurt and I had a narrative rolling around in my head that I was not good enough. The story in my head was more challenging than some of the behavioral changes I needed to make because that failure story was always being told in the back of my head, no matter what I did or how successful I was. I was abusing myself, telling myself over and over again that I was worthless, so, of course, that was how I treated others. The challenging part of my work was that the narrative drove my behavior, and I could not change one without the other.

> **The story in my head was more challenging than some of the behavioral changes I needed to make because that failure story was always being told in the back of my head, no matter what I did or how successful I was.**

The first step I had to take was to decide to deal with the hardest and ugliest part of myself, and that was my anger. My anger was so volatile and emotionally charged that it was a part of myself that I hated. From that point of shame, I did not want to even think about it. But at 17, I knew I needed help and had to do something. I had a friend at the time who knew I was struggling and invited me to a weekend self-exploration workshop.

The first workshop I went to was a

three-day affair in the early 1970s, a Werner Erhard EST training that was all about self-reflection. On day one, I was talking about my anger, and the facilitator told me in what I thought was a very condescending voice, "Bill, you must embrace your anger." I looked at him with ugliness in my eyes, and with a clenched fist, I pointed at the facilitator and said, "Why don't you embrace my anger!"

That was on the first day. What I learned by day three was that if I can't embrace that which I don't like about myself, I will not work to change it. As long as I judged, shamed, and blamed myself, I would not find the compassion to look deep enough to make any changes. I had to accept myself, in order to be able to make the changes needed to live a richer and fuller life. To accept myself, I had to be willing to go to the origination point.

A lack of will and utter ignorance of the origination point made me a slave to my judgment, shame, blame, and biases. Judgment, shame, and blame had total control over all of my interactions in my life and fueled the destructive narrative in my head. That narrative in my

> **That narrative in my head consistently manifested as destructive actions toward myself and others. Without understanding the origination point, I allowed my judgment, shame, blame, and biases to completely control all of the interactions in my life while blaming the other person.**

head consistently manifested as destructive actions toward myself and others. Without understanding the origination point, I allowed my judgment, shame, blame, and biases to completely control all of the interactions in my life while blaming the other person.

Think deeply about your own story as you embark on finding the origination point for a bias you have.

Chapter 4 Daily Reflective Practice
Origination Point

This practice is about examining a judgment or bias and seeing if you can trace it back to the origination point. Think about a bias that you have today and how it shows up. Typically, how you describe the judgment or bias today is not the origination point. I knew a person who described a bias against people who drink due to growing up in a home with an alcoholic father. This person thought it was only about people who drink and over time connected drinking to the origination point of childhood. Getting closer to the origination point, this person got more specific in that the bias was not about people who drink, but about fathers who do not provide security and care for their children. Once there was an understanding of the origination point, this person could go into the healing process. Much like my own life, the experience with an alcoholic parent was one of insecurity and lack of care, and that insecurity was the true origination point for this person's judgment and bias against people who drink.

It is important to find an entry point into this conversation and use the personal agreements you created to facilitate the conversation. You could start with a bias you are aware of. I have a bias against bad drivers, and I could start there. Think about a bias that allows you to stay in the process without throwing you into the panic zone. Gently push yourself into your learning zone.

The bias or judgment you describe is something that gets you emotionally charged. It could be a judgment or fear that you have about other people or a situation that gets you upset and emotionally charged. Usually, the biased experience that you experience today is emotionally charged and reflective of something that happened when you were younger because most of our biases are created between birth and adolescence.

I shared my story about my bias that all men are mean due to my experience with my dad. I took his behavior, extrapolated that behavior to all men, and created a bias that all men are mean. When I would meet a man, I would treat him just as I had my dad. My bias completely inhibited my ability to be in authentic relationship with men for a long time.

Take your time processing through this practice, and have conversations with your accountability partner. As you explore the origination point of a bias, be kind to yourself, and be honest about how you felt and how the bias is affecting your life today. Have a conversation with a friend or loved one about how you feel through this process. We will revisit the origination point and bias awareness later in the book. In the next chapter, we will talk about the importance of and the process for having purposeful conversations.

After engaging in my own work for a number of years, I figured out that there were daily practices to change my thinking and behaviors. I now take the approach that mindset and behaviors can be changed with commitment and practice. The next few chapters will be dedicated to understanding and creating daily practices that will support you in making changes that are sustainable over time. Building skill capacity has been a major part of my personal work, including skills such as communication, listening, mindset shifts, self-protective strategies, and others. Remember that each skill is about practice and not perfection, so take the time to intentionally work with each practice and skill until you begin to feel comfortable using them.

Each skill is about practice and not perfection.

"

A purposeful conversation is designed to be intentional and to focus on the desired outcomes that are important to you.

"

"All the world is full of suffering. It is also full of overcoming."

—Helen Keller

Chapter 5

Purposeful Conversations

To do this work, I had to figure out how to talk about my judgments and biases productively. By "productively," I mean having a conversation that was not demeaning to myself or others or that supported the negative feelings I had about myself. The patterns of communication I learned in my youth were very negative and were reflected in the harsh ways I thought about myself and the way I interacted with people. Learning the components of having a purposeful conversation helped me look within and have an internal dialogue that supported my growth. Once I was able to internalize the conversations, I could practice having purposeful conversations with other people.

The design of a purposeful conversation is wrapped around answering four questions to set up the conversation.

A purposeful conversation is designed to be intentional and to focus on the desired outcomes that are important to you. There are four questions to ask in a purposeful conversation, and we will go over them step by step. The purposeful conversation model can be used for small groups or large group meetings, and with formal and informal conversation. Formal use is done by intentionally writing down the answer to each question and making sure you are clear about your intention in the conversation with another person. I use the process informally by answering the questions in my head with self-talk or in an intentional conversation with a friend about my own growth work.

A purposeful conversation is important because people are busy and time is precious. If you ask a person or a group of people to gather and meet, it is important to make sure that the gathering and dialogue are relevant and meaningful. I can get anyone to engage with me in conversation once, but people may not be drawn to re-engage unless I provide purpose, relevance, and meaning. Engaging your own personal work and in your own conversations about judgments, bias, and your life experiences takes planning, and this purposeful conversation template is a great way to add meaning to any conversation.

Purposeful Conversation Steps

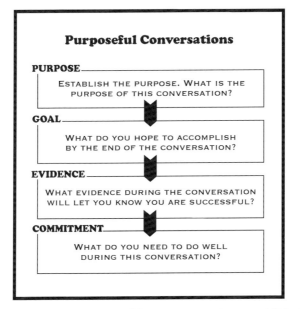

The first step in a purposeful conversation is to establish the purpose of the conversation or gathering. What is the topic you want to cover, why are you bringing a person/people together for conversation, and how are you going to describe this to the person/people you invite?

Another element of this first step is to ask permission to open the conversation, or to invite the other person or people into the conversation. How many times has someone wanted to have a conversation with you, and you really did not have the time or ability to pay attention because of your

> **Thinking about what you want to accomplish before going through the conversation allows you to make minor adjustments as you go through the conversation.**

own distractions? Were you able to say, "I don't have time right now," or did you listen distractedly and resent the time you spent with that person? Being present in the conversation is important, so limiting the distractions is important as a speaker and listener.

Establishing the purpose is also a way for you to evaluate the importance and relevance of the conversation. When planning a personal growth conversation, you can answer these questions to plan your own process. As a lone participant in my work, I was also a vocal detractor and supporter in my head. At this point of my growth, I was still using the demeaning narrative to drive my interactions. Being purposeful allowed me to start building the tools and habits of personal change.

If you are working with others in your planning, you can answer these questions as a team to drive purpose and intentionality.

Purposeful conversations support personal change, so remember to use this first step as the hook to keep yourself and others engaged in the conversation.

The second step is to ask yourself what you hope to accomplish through the conversation. I say through the conversation because regardless of the content, you can accomplish other things through a conversation.

This step is thinking about the content of your conversation and the way you want to convey your message. I have had really good messages that got completely lost because of my delivery method. After I started yelling, the only focus of the conversation was my tone of voice, body language, and behavior while the original message was lost.

If I am having a conversation with my child about getting home on time, what I hope to accomplish is to come to an agreement about a curfew and have my child be responsible when he or she is out. Once I have defined the desired outcomes, I can begin to think about how to start the conversation and how I want to act throughout the time we are talking. Through conversations, we also have the ability to create deeper relationships with each other and lower the level of fear when in conversation with the other person or people. Regardless of the content, think about the ability to build deeper relationships with everyone you interact with. With the example of the conversation with my child about being home on time, I am supporting accountability, encouraging timeliness, and deepening my relationship with my child at the same time.

Thinking about what you want to accomplish before going through the

> **Once I have defined the desired outcomes, I can begin to think about how to start the conversation and how I want to act throughout the time we are talking.**

Photo © Tina Schuler

> Being purposeful is having the ability to be continually aware of when I am judging, when I am internally distracted, or when I am making up a story about the person.

conversation allows you to make minor adjustments as you go through the conversation. Your purpose provides a skill to keep on track with the point of your conversations, which should always include getting to know each other more authentically.

The third step of a purposeful conversation is to ask yourself, what evidence during the conversation will lead you to know that you have been successful? The answer will vary based on your audience and the intent of the conversation. When I am facilitating a workshop, my success is based on audience participation, attitude, and body language.

This will look very different when I am talking to a friend or family member, and yet it is critically important to stay aware of the level of engagement in each conversation.

> **For a personal conversation, the success will be rooted in expression, being present, and being willing to hear from the other person reflectively and honestly.**

For a personal conversation, the success will be rooted in expression, being present, and being willing to hear from the other person reflectively and honestly. Being purposeful is having the ability to be aware of when I am judging, being internally distracted, or making up a story about the person.

The final step is to ask yourself what you want to be sure you do well during the conversation. This is where you decide what you need to do to make sure that you hear and that you are heard. What you want to do well is about being aware and using behaviors and skills such as paying attention, being present, staying engaged, reflecting the input you hear, asking questions, and any other behaviors you believe are important to support your communication. This step is designed to help you develop the behaviors you would like to see utilized in a conversation with another person.

All of these steps combined create a purposeful conversation that will support you in getting your message across. We will follow up by giving you an opportunity to practice having purposeful conversations before moving on to our listening process.

A manager I worked with tested the purposeful conversation model by putting together a purposeful conversation with her supervisor. She was testing the model to see if it really worked and had scheduled the meeting for 30 minutes. The night before, she answered the four questions for a purposeful conversation. The next day, she went in to speak with her boss prepared and ready to go. She told me that by using the purposeful conversation model, they were finished with the business part of the meeting in 17 minutes. They used the last 13 minutes to deepen their personal relationship with each other. The manager went on to tell me that she used the informal purposeful conversation model with her husband, and they have been having deeper and more rewarding conversations since beginning to use the model.

Chapter 5 Daily Reflective Practice
Purposeful Conversation

Set up and practice a purposeful conversation with your accountability partner about an origination point of one of your biases. Practice answering all four questions before the conversation and use them to guide you throughout the conversation. Pick a bias that is relevant to your personal understanding and growth wherever you are in your own personal work. Use the formal practice by writing down the answers to all four questions before jumping into the conversation. The practice of the origination point is to talk about a bias you currently have. Connect that bias back to a point in your past to discover the origination point and to understand how that original emotionally charged reaction—the origination point—is currently affecting your interactions with people.

This work is about practice and not perfection.

Photo © Will Dickey

> ❞
>
> "Acceptance of what has happened is the first step to overcoming the consequences of any misfortune."
>
> —William James

Chapter 6

Deep Listening

Take a moment to reflect on the purposeful conversation model and your success in structuring the conversation. What worked well and what challenged you in the design and implementation of a purposeful conversation? As we move into the next chapter, we will talk about a skill base that helped me to deepen my work at a more conscious level.

We don't often intentionally work on deep listening, because we are practicing listening all the time. Deep listening is a vital aspect and skill for an effective purposeful conversation. Listening is a skill that, with practice, we can use intentionally in our daily communications. As with a purposeful conversation, listening has steps that can be

> **When I got to this point of wanting to quit, I had to circle back frequently to why I was doing this to/for myself. I was not always sure that making the world a more humane place was truly my Why.**

used to maximize our interaction. The following steps are important to being fully engaged and deeply listening to the other person.

At this halfway point of the book, I want to tell you how I got through some of the challenges I had while doing my own personal work. There were many times when I wanted to give up and stop, and, based on my past patterns of behavior, quitting would be the "right" thing to do. Personal growth was a lot of work, and at this point, I was challenged a lot to keep going every day. I want you to remember where you landed in creating your Why.

When I got to this point of wanting to quit, I had to circle back frequently to why I was doing this to/for myself. I was not always sure that making the world a more humane place was truly my Why. When I moved myself out of despair, I realized that I could go on, and I knew the Why of being more compassionate and empathetic was indeed worth what I was going through.

Deep Listening Model
Key Tasks

Clear Deep Conversations
KEY TASKS

BE AWARE OF JUDGMENTS THAT LEAD TO BLAME/SHAME	RESPOND, DO NOT REACT
ACCEPT WHAT OTHERS HAVE TO SAY	BREATHE AND PAUSE BEFORE RESPONDING
MAINTAIN REFLECTION	SUPPORT HEALING EVEN WHEN EMOTIONALLY CHARGED

Awareness of Judgment That Leads to Blame or Shame

The first step to becoming a deep listener is to listen outside of judgment that leads to blame or shame. This means that you are listening for meaning and are an undistracted and willing participant in the conversation. From this place, you are aware of how judgment is affecting the interaction. Deep listening entails letting go of the judgment that can lead to blame or shame. Remember that, for us as humans, it is

> **When I drop into judgment, I drop out of being present because I am engaged in the interaction based on the story and my judgment of the other person or his or her behavior.**

impossible not to judge, so this is not about stopping yourself from judging, discerning, or thinking about things throughout the conversation.

This agreement is about being more present in a conversation and not allowing your judgment to guide your responses. When I drop into judgment, I drop out of being present because I am engaged in the interaction based on the story and my judgment of the other person or his or her behavior. Being aware of judgment is about heightening your level of self-awareness so that when you drop into judgment, you are aware of the judgment, let it go, and come back to be present in the conversation.

Response or Reaction

The next step is to assess whether you are responsive or reactive in the conversation. Have you ever been in a conversation where you were thinking about what you wanted to say before the other person was done speaking? If you answered yes to this question, you are a normal human being, because we are all socialized to behave in this way in a conversation. What I learned in doing my own work is that if I am thinking about what I want to say before the other person is done talking, I should say, "What you are saying is kind of interesting. But I am not listening to you anymore, and I am ready to tell you what I think." We would not say that, though, would we? We would not say that because that would be rude, and yet in my brain, I am completely disengaged from the other person.

When my brain kicks in to think about what I want to say before the other person is done talking, I am no longer able to listen. Once I start thinking about what I want to say, my ability to deeply listen is overruled by my desire to react and say something. What I need to say may or may not even be connected to what the other person is talking about, which is why I call this state of being "mind chatter."

Think about the times you have been in conversation with someone and decided what you wanted to say before that person was done talking. Do you find yourself antsy and wanting the other person to stop talking so you can say what you want to say? Do you start to talk the moment they have closed their mouths? Do you interrupt because you have something to say right away? Most of us are socialized to communicate in a way that is engaging and affirming, and we make a lot of assumptions about nonverbal cues. All of the distractions in my brain that take away my attention in a conversation are called reactions, and that is about me. If I listen, don't interrupt, ask questions, and reflect, I am going to be more responsive, and the response will be connected

> **Thinking about what you want to accomplish before going through the conversation allows you to make minor adjustments as you go through the conversation.**

to the person I am talking to. In deep listening, a reaction to the other person is about me and a response is about the other person.

So if you catch yourself creating a reaction before the other person is done talking, you can let go of your thought and return your attention to the person as quickly as you can. If you cannot consistently be present and focus on what the person is saying, you can tell him or her, "I really want to hear what you have to say, but my brain is thinking about something else, so I am not currently present, and I need a moment to refocus. Will you pause a moment for me, or can we take a break?" Then finish your distracting thought and return your attention to the speaker. Other people may be so honored that you're so committed to giving them quality attention that they will be willing to give you a break to recompose yourself. As you practice this technique over time, you will be able to recreate this process in your head. As you do that, you will move from being less reactive to being more responsive in the moment without having to take a break or ending the conversation.

Accept What Others Have to Say

This is important to me because, for a long time, I would not accept anything anyone else had to say unless it matched what I thought was right. When I was living from an ego-driven perspective, I was concerned only with how things affected me, and I would judge other people unless they agreed with me. It took me a long time to understand that my truth is not the truth and that I could accept other people's truths if I let go of the need to be right.

Acceptance outside of judgment means that I can hear a truth different from mine and accept what is being said. This acceptance does not mean that I agree with what is being said, and my lack of agreement does not make the other person bad or wrong. I may not agree with what is being said, and if I am operating with the working agreements of awareness of judgment that leads to blame or shame, I have no right to make the other person wrong.

> **Acceptance outside of judgment means that I can hear a truth different from mine and accept what is being said.**

Breathe and Pause Before Responding

Breath and pause are about heightening awareness about self-care when one gets emotionally charged in the conversation. Taking a pause and a breath when emotionally charged allows you a moment's time to de-escalate the charge and decide how to re-engage in the conversation. Breathing and pausing are techniques that can be used to help process

> **This difference is between blaming the other person through being a triggered victim or owning the role you play in the conversation.**

emotionally charged reactions to what is being said and give you a moment to process why the emotional charge exists. I don't want to react to those highly energetic, emotionally charged reactions and run the risk of hurting someone.

These breathing and pausing techniques allow you a moment to gain more clarity. Taking a breath, pausing, and asking questions are ways that help me to process the emotion without having my emotions negatively affect the conversation. What are some self-care strategies you can use when you get emotionally charged?

Reflection

This element of deep listening is asking you to stay centered and present for another person. Stay in self-reflection so that you are aware of the mind chatter and so that you can gauge whether you are reactive or responsive. Reflect on when you drop into judgment or bias so that you can pull yourself back and stay present. A reflection allows you to see yourself while you are remaining aware of where the other person is and how he or she is feeling throughout your conversations.

Support Healing While
Being Emotionally Charged

Having lived half of my life as a triggered victim who was emotionally charged, I had to change something to shift that approach as part of this journey. I learned that when I became emotionally charged, I became a victim. As a victim, I was blaming other people for what happened to me, and then I got mad at them. Over time, I learned that there is a difference between living as a victim and learning to own my stuff.

This difference is between blaming the other person through being a triggered victim or owning the role you play in the conversation. Have you ever been in a conversation with someone where you were rolling merrily along, and all of a sudden that person seemed irrational to you? One of those conversations where you walk away and say, "What just happened?" This behavior is a good example of someone who is emotionally charged.

Think about the circumstances of the conversation and what happened during and after that person got emotionally charged. Typically, the person would say that he or she was irrational because something you did triggered him or her into reacting like that.

In essence, what people are saying when they say, "Something you did triggered me," is that something you did caused them to act like that, and you should apologize and recognize how hurtful you are. What they are doing is deflecting any responsibility from themselves and blaming you for their emotional reaction.

From the position of being triggered, they want to remain a victim, and then they will victimize you by telling you to fix it. If they have enough power over you or they are a bully or someone who leads by fear, you will be compliant. Have you ever been in a compliant relationship where you just did what you were told and were unsure of the other person? What was the impact on you while you were in that compliant relationship?

You can allow the person to remain a victim if you respond defensively. A response such as "I did not say that," "I did not mean to say that," or "You are taking it out of context" sets up a dynamic where you are trying to make the other person feel emotionally better, which is impossible. I cannot make you feel better if you choose not to by how I respond to you if you are emotionally charged about something happening in our interaction.

I learned to understand this from a mentor of mine 25 years ago, and the perspective has helped me more than I ever thought it would. My mentor talked about a process called a restimulated emotional experience.

A restimulated emotional experience is when what is happening now in a current interaction causes someone to become emotionally charged and irrational due to the restimulation of a painful emotional experience from the past. The current interaction is simply acting as a trigger rather than the actual cause.

> **From the position of being triggered, they want to remain a victim, and then they will victimize you by telling you to fix it.**

This emotionally charged restimulation is connected to a traumatic unhealed experience that is being conveyed through the words I am using, coupled with body language, tonality of voice, or some other stimuli. The reason we walk away from one of these conversations and wonder what just happened is that we do not know if the other person went back to last week, last month, last year, or 10 years ago.

When we are restimulated, we can drop into that victim mentality that says the problem is something outside of ourselves, or we can choose to own what is happening. If I am involved with you at the time, I have a choice about how to respond. I can let you remain a triggered victim, or I can support your ownership of the emotional charge, which could lead you to a healing process.

The process of ownership is different from the process of

> **This restimulated experience process is about understanding that throughout this work, you will get emotionally stimulated, and an emotional charge or restimulation is an indicator of more personal work to be done.**

a triggered victim. If I treat you as a triggered victim, I will try to make you feel better. If I understand that what is happening is a restimulated experience, my response will be different. I might say something like "Is everything okay? Because I noticed something has changed in our interaction." Or, I might say that I noticed an emotional charge in our interaction and ask if there is something else we need to talk about. I might ask if it is necessary for us to take a break. I don't want to label the emotional charge as good or bad or as anger, because as soon as I label your emotion, I have judged you and our conversations will change. When we feel judged in the conversation, one person will be defensive, and the other person will justify why he or she is correct.

I do not want to divorce myself from the interaction, and I also do not want to own anything that is not mine. If I did something to hurt or denigrate you, then I will have to own that, and if you are getting emotionally restimulated based on your own past experiences, I want to support you in processing those feelings if you are willing.

This restimulated experience process is about understanding that throughout this work, you will get emotionally stimulated, and an emotional charge or restimulation is an indicator of more personal work to be done. Throughout the growth process, I am asking you to bring up unhealed experiences from your past and relive them, so that you can start a healing process that allows you to move forward.

Throughout the bias conversation, you may get restimulated, especially if someone shares a bias about you that is unseen. I worked with a group facilitating a bias conversation, and one of the women said that she had a bias against moms who stay at home. There was a woman in the circle who immediately started crying, and she felt an emotional charge. She had been a working mom, and, due to health circumstances, she had had to become a stay-at-home mom. The bias that was shared is that if you are a stay-at-home mom, your worth is less than that of a working mother.

The person who shared this bias was not intending to hurt the other person and did not know the circumstances behind the other mom staying at home. As the stay-at-home mom got more emotionally stimulated, she shared through tears and pains her story about how she became a stay-at-home mom. It was a great breakthrough for the stay-at-home mom because she had never shared her story or that level of emotion about her situation. The person who had that bias was able to understand that not all stay-at-home moms match the experience that she had had with them.

The person with the bias learned something new about her colleague, and they shared a very rich, deep, and meaningful conversation. This experience allowed them both to take their relationship to a deeper level, and the emotional exchange benefitted all the people in this circle.

Deep Listening Skill: Reflecting

One of the strategies you can use if you get distracted from deep listening is called reflective listening. When your own mind chatter gets the best of your attention, reflective listening can bring your attention back to the speaker. All you do is reflect back to the speaker what you are hearing. The process of reflective listening allows you to get centered, to ground yourself with the speaker, and to make sure you are attentive to his or her train of thought. Supporting another person to make sure he or she is able to share a full train of thought is a key outcome of reflective listening.

Mirroring is a simple form of reflecting, and it involves repeating what the speaker says. Mirroring should be succinct and reflect what you have heard, but it should not always be a verbatim response to what was said. It is helpful to reflect on the expressions you heard before you got distracted. (If they say, "I'm angry that I feel stuck here!" you can mirror by saying, "You feel angry and stuck.") This mirroring allows you to let the speaker know that you are doing your best to stay connected to him or her. Mirroring can also allow the speaker to continue without hijacking his or her train of thought.

Another strategy to stop the mind chatter and use reflective listening is called paraphrasing. Paraphrasing is about using words to reflect what you are hearing from the other person. Paraphrasing shows that you are listening and making an effort to deeply understand what the other person is saying. You are not parroting back what is being said; instead, you're summarizing and using your intuition

The process of reflective listening allows you to get centered, to ground yourself with the speaker, and to make sure you are attentive to his or her train of thought.

and asking questions to gain clarity about what the other person is saying and what is affecting him or her the most.

Your paraphrasing responses should be open ended and nonjudgmental, and you may be challenged to ask questions until you become more skilled using this technique. The other person might say, "No, that is not what I said," and that means you need to go back to deep listening and ask reflective questions.

One of the outcomes of mirroring and paraphrasing is that they can give you and the other person time to regroup and refocus. Reflecting other people in a conversation can help them stay focused in their experience and gain new insights. You can build this skill if you take the time to practice and use the techniques infused into deep listening and purposeful conversations.

An inquiry-based model is another important concept to use when engaged in deep listening with another person. An inquiry-based model is where you ask questions that allow you to stay connected and get real information from the other person. Asking questions also allows the other person to stay fully in his or her train of thought to make sure he or she is able to fully share without distractions.

Some examples of distractions are the following:

- Cell phone—should be silenced and out of sight
- Computer and other electronics
- Music
- Preoccupation about something else you have to do or are thinking about
- Other people in the room
- Room environment—warm or cold, light or dark
- Objects in your hands
- Judgment that you are unable to release toward the other person

Chapter 6 Daily Reflective Practice
Deep Listening

❧

Deep listening is a skill that I have been practicing since I was 18, and it is still hard work. The process I am sharing with you has to be done with your accountability partner or someone else who is willing to do a deep listening practice. This is going to be a timed process, and you will each have two minutes to talk. The prompt you are going to talk about is the following: Why is this work of value to you? Why did you choose to read this book and engage in a process of increased self-awareness? What is the value of getting to know yourself and understanding how your biases are affecting your life? What do you think the impact of this work will be on your personal life? I think that through these questions, you have enough content to talk uninterrupted for about two minutes.

Sit face to face with the other person so you can make eye contact with him or her away from a table or anything that creates a physical divide between you. There is only one rule for this process, and that is for the listener. As a listener, you can breathe, and you can blink. For the listener, there is no head nodding, no smiling, no eye rolling, no laughing, no high-fiving, or any sharing about how you have a similar story. This is an exercise in deep listening, and for two minutes, the listener will listen impassively, which means to give no sign of feeling or emotion and provide no response.

If the speaker finishes before the two minutes are up, you will spend the last bit of time making beautiful eye contact. Remember that this is an exercise in deep listening, so I do not want you to start a conversation. After the first two minutes are up, switch so that the speaker becomes the listener and vice versa, and start the timer for another two minutes. Once the second speaker finishes, we will debrief the exercise.

Deep Listening Exercise Debrief

So how was the experience of listening impassively for two minutes? What did you feel, not being able to make any movement or give feedback? How was it for you as the speaker?

There are a couple of main responses from the speaker and the listener, and a variety of feelings in the middle. On one end, as the speaker, you may have found this process very difficult, frustrating, and hard as you spoke without getting any response. You may have found yourself questioning your own comments because you were not getting any feedback from your partner. On the other end, as the speaker, you may have felt relieved to be able to talk without any interruptions for two minutes. You may have also felt that it was hard to talk uninterrupted because you could not tell if the other person agreed or disagreed with you.

As the listener, you may have been challenged because you could not respond to anything that was being said. You may have been more engaged because you did not have to respond to anything and could just listen. Many people also find that looking into someone's eyes for that long is challenging, especially if they have run out of things to say and there is still time left on the clock.

Without the nonverbal cues, some listeners are not able to stay on track in the conversation, and some speakers are not sure if what they're saying makes sense to the other person. We have become socialized to these nonverbal cues as a way to tell us if we are making sense or are on the right track with our conversations. In essence, many of us feel that we cannot be effective in communication without assurance from the other person that what we are saying makes sense. We frequently change our train of thought based on the assumptions we are making about the other person's nonverbal cues.

How would you define an assumption? Most people

are familiar with the saying about the meaning of the word *assume* as "making an ass out of you and me." The Oxford dictionary defines an assumption as "a thing that is accepted as true or as certain to happen, without proof." An assumption is a story or belief that we create in our head about something that is happening in our interaction without any factual basis to prove it is true. Once the story comes into our heads, it becomes our truth, and we operate from that truth, even though we have no facts to support that belief. The reality and impact of our assumptions are important to notice in communication because many of our assumptions are based on nonverbal cues happening in our interactions and we embrace our assumptions as if they are facts.

If I am talking to you and nodding, smiling, and saying words that lead you to assume I am listening, you may believe that I agree with what you are saying and continue on your course based on the assumption you are making about my nonverbal cues. If in the same conversation I don't nod or you sense that I don't agree with you, receiving these nonverbal signals, you may shift your entire train of thought based on your assumption about what I am thinking.

I worked with a student doing this listening process, and he came up to me afterward and told me what he had learned about communication with his teacher. He said, "If I smile and nod my head in the affirmative, my teacher will make an assumption that I am listening and move on."

He figured out that by giving a nonverbal cue, he could actually manipulate the communication between himself and his teacher.

On the other end of the communication spectrum, when you see a look of disapproval when speaking, it could relate to a number of feelings. For example, I could have been out for a walk last night and tripped and hurt my hip. When I changed positions during our conversation, I felt so much pain that you saw me with a grimace on my face. What you are assuming from my grimace is disapproval of what you are saying, when in reality, the grimace is actually about something within myself that has nothing to do with what you said.

As a participant shared in one of my workshops, "So what you are saying is that we are manipulating and hijacking each other's train of thoughts with our nonverbals." We are using nonverbals to drive each other's train of thought consciously and unconsciously in every conversation we are having. Our reactions to our assumptions about what nonverbals mean are also constantly derailing us. The question to ask from this perspective is, what level of nonverbal cues can I give you to let you know that I am still engaged without manipulating your train of thought?

I am not advocating for this style of impassive listening in our conversation because it's impossible to eradicate our socialization process of how we communicate. What I am advocating for is a higher level of self-awareness when we engage with another person in a conversation.

Self-awareness is the ability to remain conscious in your daily interactions and emotions of self and others. Self-awareness allows you to stay present and evaluate an interaction based in reality so that you are aware of your effect on others and self.

Hallmarks of self-awareness include self-confidence, realistic self-assessment, and a self-deprecating sense of humor. Levels of self-awareness depend on one's ability to monitor one's own emotional state and to correctly identify the feelings associated with each interaction.

◆ Self-awareness allows you to build self-confidence to be able to accurately self-assess your emotional awareness.

◆ Self-managing is about being aware of the behaviors and actions you are using in relationships. Trust, being conscientious, and having motivation and ambition are all a part of self-managing.

◆ Cultural awareness is about understanding the environment in which you interact and being able to maneuver through the many nuances of those interactions. Cultural awareness also brings into consciousness the elements, beliefs, and values of society. Cultural awareness allows you to understand the differences in communication styles and approaches to dialogue.

◆ Relational awareness enables you to build the capacity to inspire and mentor others. This is also a framework for building a strong team that collaborates effectively with each other.

Social-emotional intelligence enables you to build capacity in problem solving, critical thinking, communication, and conflict resolution. Building my social-emotional intelligence has been a key driver of my learning and ability to change. As you go through the practices in this book, you will be building your social-emotional intelligence in ways that will support continued growth and awareness.

Hijacking Train of Thought

When two people engage in a conversation, there is a purpose for why they are coming together to talk. Someone has a train of thought that he or she wants to share with another person, so he or she initiates a conversation. When I am engaged with someone, and that person has a train of thought, I can hijack that train of thought with nonverbal cues. When people are talking, their train of thought is like a straight line, and I can do what is culturally normal and say something like, "Oh yeah, I did that too. Here is what I did …" I have just taken their train of thought, and now they have to follow me. They may never feel heard, they may never get back to what brought us into the conversation, but I may walk away thinking what a great conversation it had been. The other person may feel devalued because of how

I treated him or her and may not even tell me or may avoid having conversations with me in the future, because of how I took his or her train of thought and made it mine.

The questions I encourage you to ponder about your communication habits are the following: What types of nonverbal responses can you use to let the other person know that you are present and engaged without manipulating or trying to hijack his or her train of thought? Are you reactive, by allowing the mind chatter to get in the way of deep listening, or are you listening and asking questions, gaining clarity, and crafting a thoughtful response to what you are hearing? While I am not advocating for people to listen impassively and not make nonverbal cues, I am going to make some suggestions about how we can communicate more effectively. Remember that a mind chatter reaction is about me, and a crafted response is about the other person. If we build skills that allow us to be more responsive, we can start appreciating and understanding each other more deeply, and grow closer because of it. Even conflict can bring us closer together if we know how to listen to each other. When participants in a workshop understand the need for deep listening, the next question is typically, "How should I engage with someone if I can't listen impassively and want to satisfy the human desire to be engaged?"

If I am in a conversation with you and I want to satisfy that human urge to be engaged, there is an approach that can be taken to ensure that the other person stays in his or her train of thought, without being hijacked by you. You can use an inquiry-based model in your conversations, which entails asking questions to gain greater clarity and understanding. An inquiry-based model allows to you be engaged in the conversation while deepening your self-awareness about how you are engaged with the other person. While you're listening and asking questions, you can notice whether your nonverbal and verbal responses are detracting from or supporting the other person to stay in his or her train of thought until he or she is complete.

You can ask a series of questions that allow the other person to go deeper into his or her train of thought, so the process benefits both the speaker and the listener.

Some examples of questions that allow for the conversation to deepen are the following:

- ◆ That sounds really interesting. How did that affect you?
- ◆ What did that experience tell you about yourself?
- ◆ How has that affected you as you have grown?
- ◆ Tell me, what is the most important point for me to hear in our conversation?
- ◆ How is the experience you shared connected to our conversation today?
- ◆ How does this feel for you?

The point of asking questions is to allow you to satisfy that urge to be engaged in the other person's conversation, without interjecting your train of thought too early into the conversation. This approach supports the speaker to stay engaged in his or her train of thought long enough to be complete. At a certain point, you will intuitively know the other person is complete, or he or she will invite you into the conversation by asking you what you think.

Using the inquiry-based model described, you will have a lot of information with which to respond to the other person in a way that shows you listened and you care. At the same time, you are aware that when you drop into judgment, it may cause you to check out. This can help you let judgment go and allow you to come back to be present. The deep listening practice is designed to support you in being aware of the impact of your assumptions on nonverbal cues. It helps you gather real and clear information about what the other person is saying without hijacking his or her train of thought and continues deepening your state of self-awareness when in conversation with another person.

When you think about the process you completed with the purposeful conversation model and couple it with deep listening, how would you answer the following questions?

- ◆ How can purposeful conversations and deep listening affect a relationship?
- ◆ How can purposeful conversations and deep listening help the speaker with the conversation?

Have a conversation with your accountability partner and talk about what you think and any new awareness that has come to you through your understanding of purposeful conversations and deep listening.

Thich Nhat Hanh stated, "Deep listening is the kind of listening that can help relieve the suffering of another person. You can call it compassionate listening. You listen with only one purpose: to help him or her to empty his heart."

On one Super Soul Sunday, Thich Nhat Hanh had a conversation with Oprah about compassionate listening. If you are able to view this brief video online, have a conversation with your accountability partner about the feelings and thoughts that came up for you as you watched this video on deep compassionate listening.

Chapter 6 Daily Reflective Practice
Deep Listening 2

❧

Think about something you want to improve in your deep listening practices. Is it to be more aware of your judgments, to listen more deeply, to get closer to other people, to be more responsive and less reactive? This practice is designed to build your skill base with deep listening. As an example, I will share with you the daily practice that has supported me for many years to enhance my listening practices.

I realized years ago that I was a very reactive listener. I would interrupt people and steal their train of thought, and I felt like I was a great listener. I thought I had a lot of great things to say, and as long as people were quiet, I could give them the benefit of my wisdom. Through my own work, I grew to understand that I had to improve my listening practices and that I do not have all the answers.

I started my listening process years ago, and it was really challenging at first. Over the years, it has become easier, and at times I am not even aware that I am doing it. For me to improve my listening ability, I had to introduce new skills, and that is what I did. When I am in conversation with other people, I am repeating all of their words in my head as they speak, because if I repeat their words in my head, there is less room for me to fill my head with my own judgments or reactionary responses. As I am processing everything that they are saying, this allows me to craft questions that allow for deeper understanding. This inquiry process helps the speakers to get clearer about their message. Through this deep listening and using the inquiry-based process, I am able to be responsive based on the messages I am hearing from the speaker.

> **Daily practices are designed to give you alternatives to limiting behaviors, and this work is about practice and not perfection.**

A *reminder*: Daily practices are designed to give you alternatives to limiting behaviors, and this work is about practice and not perfection. As you think about what you want to change, look at yourself honestly and think about what the hardest aspect of listening is for you. Start there. If you can take on that which is hardest or most scary, the rest is more manageable.

Use your journal to write about your listening skill base, and what practice you want to change. Track your daily practice the same way you would track any kind of workout. How much time were you able to sit and practice today? How did judgment show up, and what was the impact on your interaction? Were you able to let go of the judgment and come back and be present? Did the other person seem to feel deeply heard by you? Congratulate and praise yourself when you achieve your goals. Be kind and compassionate to yourself when you fall short of your goals, and continue to practice.

For me to improve my listening ability, I had to introduce new skills, and that is what I did. When I am in conversation with other people, I am repeating all of their words in my head as they speak, because if I repeat their words in my head, there is less room for me to fill my head with my own judgments or reactionary responses.

—— **,,** ——
We were literally dancing
around the triangle, shifting
roles and creating drama
within each movement.

Photo © Boris H. Pophristov

> "Believe you can and you're halfway there."
>
> —Theodore Roosevelt

Chapter 7

Drama Triangle

In this chapter, we will continue to look at the ways that we protect ourselves from engaging in deep conversations due to patterns of behavior created over time. To begin, let's reflect on the practices you have completed up to this point. How was your listening process, and what did you learn throughout the deep listening process? Have any thoughts or behaviors started changing as a result of your practices? Have you created practices that are replicable and support you in deeper learning and understanding of how you operate? How have you connected purposeful conversations to a deep listening practice? Are you using your personal agreements, and how is that process serving you?

Celebrate your accomplishments and follow through more effectively with commitments that are not having the desired outcome.

———— 🙦 ————

Being a victim was a self-protective behavior I used and enhanced to keep me safe from the other person.

One of those default behaviors I created when emotionally charged was to blame the other person for what was happening to me and from there play the victim and subsequently persecute the other as a cycle of behavior.

We are going to start this chapter with a look at something that has helped me to understand where I go when I get thrown. "Getting thrown" means that when I am interacting with someone and I get emotionally charged from the interaction, I get thrown off balance. When I get emotionally charged, I run the risk of getting thrown and knocked off balance by the interaction. When I am emotionally charged and thrown, that is an indication of a need for more internal work if I am not playing the victim.

Being a victim was a self-protective behavior I used and enhanced to keep me safe from the other person. One of those default behaviors I created when emotionally charged was to blame the other person for what was happening to me and from there play the victim and subsequently persecute the other person as a cycle of behavior.

When I was a young, ego-driven victim, I blamed everyone for being thrown, for how I felt, and I thought that I could make them wrong so they would change.

If they did not change, then I figured that they were, in fact, wrong, and I would not engage with them. What I now understand is that what I was doing was getting on the Drama Triangle as a victim and persecutor. The Drama Triangle also contains the rescuer role, and when I went to rescuer, it was to prove that I was right and that I knew the answer for the other person. As we explore the Karpman Drama Triangle, think about where you go and what kinds of emotional charges throw you to get you on the triangle. Through this process, we will also talk about techniques you can use to get yourself off of the triangle.

"Getting thrown" means that when I am interacting with someone and I get emotionally charged from the interaction, I get thrown off balance. When I get emotionally charged, I run the risk of getting thrown and knocked off balance by the interaction.

Karpman's Drama Triangle

The Drama Triangle depicts a model of dysfunctional and default behavioral actions that we take when we are thrown from an emotionally charged interaction. At each point of the triangle and between the triangles are areas for an ineffective response to conflict. The points on the triangle represent the victim, persecutor, and rescuer. While on the triangle, I perpetuate dysfunctional default behaviors, thoughts, and actions similar to the thoughts, behaviors, and actions I outlined in my initial self-assessment. The triangle depicts communication methods we use, and there are ways to act that help to avoid the Drama Triangle.

Dr. Stephen Karpman developed the Drama Triangle in order to visually portray the complicated interactions that occur between participants when they are entangled in conflict. It details how those participants in conflict move among the three roles/points of his Drama Triangle. Dr. Karpman developed his Drama Triangle while studying under Eric Berne, MD, the founder of transactional analysis.

When I am within the triangle of drama, I look at the experience through the lens of winner and loser. I am the winner, and the other person is the loser.

Transactional analysis is defined as a system of popular psychology based on the idea that one's behavior and social relationships reflect an interchange among parental (critical and nurturing), adult (rational), and childlike (intuitive and dependent) aspects of personality established early in life. These behaviors have created biases that are reflected throughout our lives and that have the potential to get restimulated in our current interactions. These restimulated interactions have the potential to throw me off, which knocks me off balance, and I jump on the triangle.

Understanding what throws me and where I go when I am on the Drama Triangle will support me in making personal changes when I am emotionally charged.

Understanding what throws me and where I go when I am on the Drama Triangle will support me in making personal changes when I am emotionally charged. I have created many conflicts while moving through the triangle and blaming others for my internal emotionally charged behaviors. I deflected my own feelings onto the other person and then, while unconscious, kept myself on the triangle. This triangle deflection caused me to blame the outside stimulus instead of looking at the internal emotions that were the origination of my emotionally charged experiences.

The Drama Triangle of Dr. Karpman is shown here. The P stands for persecutor, the R stands for rescuer, and the V stands for victim.

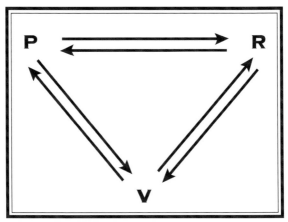

Dr. Stephen Karpman's Drama Triangle. Used with permission.
www.KarpmanDramaTriangle.com

When I am within the triangle of drama, I look at the experience through the lens of winner and loser. I am the winner, and the other person is the loser. Whether I am the victim, persecutor, or rescuer, I see myself as the good guy and the other person as the bad guy. When I am on the triangle, I get even more drawn in, even seduced, by the energy that the drama generates. The drama obscures the real issues and confusion, and upset escalates. While on the triangle, I create chaos, and while I am in the chaos, solutions that are rational, win-win, or about the relationship are no longer my focus.

When I drop into the Drama Triangle, I am no longer aware of how I am behaving because I am unconscious and my energy is focused outward as a victim, rescuer, or persecutor.

In the triangle, I play all three roles from an ego-driven perspective and do not care about what the other person is feeling or experiencing in my behavior. At the time, I was so unconscious that I had no idea I was on the triangle, and even if I had known, my skill base was so minimal that I blamed the other person and I looked at him or her as the persecutor.

Here are the descriptions of each role in the Drama Triangle.

Victim

◆ Victims sincerely feel victimized, oppressed, helpless, hopeless, powerless, and ashamed and blame other people for how they are feeling. They have a "poor me" attitude that is always looking for help and support.

◆ As a victim, I am going to blame you, and I will also want you to fix the problem. Victims do not take responsibility for their negative interactions and feel powerless to make any changes.

Persecutor

◆ Persecutors use verbal demeaning as their power. "How stupid was that." "I can't believe you just said that ridiculous thing." These are some of the ways persecutors attack. As the persecutor, I am going to act as though whatever is happening can be fixed using verbally demeaning behavior.

◆ As the persecutor, I blame and get mad at the other

person, wanting him or her to feel bad for what is happening in the interaction. I am also connected to being a victim as the persecutor, because I want the other person to be responsible for what is happening.

Rescuer

♦ Rescuers are in the saving business and have a basic belief that people are unappreciative and selfish. Rescuing has negative effects because it allows victims to remain dependent, gives them permission to fail, and continues to blame the outside stimulus. The rescuer approach can also support the other person in remaining a victim, which allows him or her to blame someone else for what is happening. Rescuers work so hard to help other people that they may become tired or sick often, or have other physical issues.

♦ As the rescuer, I drop into my ego and act as if I have the answer for other people. I will interrupt them and tell them the truth, even if they fight me. As a rescuer, I won't care about the other people or if they like my given answer, because in my head I am the hero.

When people are on the triangle, they can shift into alternate roles during the course of an interaction, and a lot of drama and conflict occurs within those shifts on the triangle. A rescuer could become a victim or persecutor throughout the interaction on the triangle. Victims need someone to save them, rescuers need someone in need, and persecutors need someone to attack.

I attracted and created a lot of drama while living on the triangle. As an unhealthy, unconscious person, I loved working the triangle and did not want to get off of it, and I was never truly happy. The work I had to do to get off the triangle started with being aware of where I was and what I wanted.

Growing up in fear meant a lot of my triangle drama was connected to not knowing if I would be beaten or verbally demeaned for being who I was. My relationship with my dad was so scary that I truly felt myself to be both a victim and a persecutor and wished for a rescuer.

As a healthier person, I drop into the triangle less and less, and I am more aware when I get on the triangle. This awareness allows me to use some of these daily practices:

- ◆ Owning my own outcomes in relationships and not playing the victim
- ◆ Awareness of judgment as a place of interaction with another person
- ◆ Listening to respond
- ◆ Accepting feedback
- ◆ Making my implicit biases explicit

If I can do these practices, my ability to stay off the triangle increases. If I do jump on the triangle, I can get myself off the triangle quickly so that I can be present, engaged, and authentic in my interactions. The Drama Triangle has been a place of deep learning for me, and I have decided that I want to stay off the triangle as much as possible.

When I was on the Drama Triangle, I started out as a victim of something happening, and I was always blaming someone or something else for it. If I was not accepted as the victim, I would move into persecutor, where I would demean and judge the other person in a very negative and condescending manner. Moving from one place on the triangle to another caused a lot of conflict for the other person and me.

We were literally dancing around the triangle, shifting roles and creating drama within each movement. When unaware, I had no idea that what I described was happening, and as I increased my self-awareness, that changed. I became more conscious of my interactions and the impacts of my behavior. I started to see how damaging my behaviors were in the relationship, but I did not know what to do to change. I found myself asking, how do I get off the triangle?

I continue to use the strategies I am sharing in this book to get myself off the triangle and am less and less the victim, persecutor, or rescuer. If you are one of those people who like drama, think about the impacts that drama is having on your life. How is that drama serving you right now, and what are the messages and behaviors that you want to change?

What do you need to do to keep yourself off of the triangle?

Dr. Karpman's latest work talks about a way to stave off the Drama Triangle by using the Compassion Triangle. This approach is designed to challenge you to think about how you want to stay in the game and be responsible and authentic with less drama. Many of the practices in this book will support you in creating a more joyful and responsible life, including getting off the Drama Triangle. The daily practices will allow you to be kinder and more responsible and stay off of the Drama Triangle, if you choose to make the changes.

The Compassion Triangle

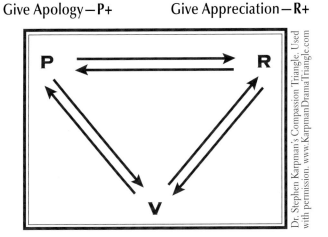

Give Apology — P+   Give Appreciation — R+

Give Sympathy — V+

Dr. Stephen Karpman's Compassion Triangle. Used with permission. www.KarpmanDramaTriangle.com

The Compassion Triangle
Three Escape Options

We started this work with a self-assessment and then went into the need for intentional and purposeful conversations. After that, we went into the importance of deep listening and the importance of building our communication skills capacity. These practices will support you in shifting your mindset, increasing your self-awareness, and over time changing your beliefs and actions while on the triangle. Bias awareness is connected to the learning steps by enabling you to get to the origination point of your negative experience.

The origination point is the place of healing and understanding. Continue to create daily practices as you move through this book and journal your steps, thoughts, and ways you want to hold yourself accountable.

The interactions I had on the triangle were very destructive, and I justified my behavior because of the childhood I had.

Chapter 7 Daily Reflective Practice
Getting Off the Drama Triangle

༺✺༻

As you examine the triangle shown here, take some time and think about the self-assessment sheet that you completed in Chapter 1. Take the self-assessment and start to link the behaviors, thoughts, and action to a place on the triangle. As you create the linkages, honestly self-reflect on the impacts you have had with other people when you are on the triangle. What were the situations, and how did the other person experience you? How did you justify your behavior as being acceptable, as the victim, persecutor, or rescuer? Take out your journal and continue to process your thinking as you engage in a purposeful conversation with your accountability partner about your experiences on the triangle.

Journal writing prompts:
- ◆ What was the situation that put you on the triangle?
- ◆ What was your role in the drama?
- ◆ How long did you stay on the triangle?
- ◆ What are your specific behaviors and thoughts when you are the victim, rescuer, or persecutor?

- ◆ What steps did you take to get off the triangle?
- ◆ How can you live in the Compassion Triangle and escape the Drama Triangle?

Example of My Reflective Practice

> **The people I attracted were also on the triangle, and we supported each other's lack of insight or growth. We sabotaged each other by commiserating with each other about how unfair life was.**

The interactions I had on the triangle were very destructive, and I justified my behavior because of the childhood I had. My parents were divorced, my dad was mean, my sister died, and I used all of these experiences to truly be and live in a victim mentality for many years. When people did not see me as a victim, I felt it was fine to persecute them. When I was young, my life felt hopeless, and I did not know what help to ask my parents for because my parents were in a chaotic place with their lives. I attracted people like me who confirmed my victim behavior by reaffirming how I had been wronged in life and how I was justified in blaming others. I lived in various roles on the triangle for about half of my life and did not have the ability to discern or know how to get off the triangle. The people I attracted were also on the triangle, and we supported each other's lack of insight or growth. We sabotaged each other by commiserating with each other about how unfair life was.

The ability to discern on any level was not a part of my narrative, and as I grew up in and on the triangle, this is what I thought was "normal," and so I replicated the behavior and actions. The ability to think about what I needed was not a part of my life, and my parents were unable to help me because they were raising me the same way they had been raised.

I went to the rescuer mode to balance my victim mode, because in my head if I could not help myself, I would help others. Many of my behaviors, reflected on the assessment I shared, put me into the victim or persecutor role, and I rescued others because of my feelings of being inept and powerless. Rescuing someone else always made me feel better even if my rescue made the other person's life worse. While it is challenging to admit this, it is important for me to see this side of myself. At first, I was in complete denial that I was a mean person because I was such a victim. This was another twisted way that I justified my victimhood and supported my big ego-driven approach to life. In being a rescuer, I hurt people because I convinced them that I was right and they trusted me to make decisions for them that did not work out. As a victim, I then blamed them for everything that had happened and

> **I understand today that I was an angry victim for the first half of my life who blamed, persecuted, and victimized other people because of my "poor me" attitude.**

would use persecution as a weapon. This approach confirms the idea that, though "thin-skinned" individuals are hurt easily, as they jump to save others, their hearts become hardened. Thin skin = hard heart; thick skin = soft heart.

I understand today that I was an angry victim for the first half of my life who blamed, persecuted, and victimized other people because of my "poor me" attitude. When I started making changes, I had to create daily practices that allowed me to stay off the Drama Triangle. An initial daily practice was to stop playing the victim and take responsibility for my thoughts, words, and actions. At the beginning, that was very hard because I still wanted to blame and shame, so I had to change my narrative and stop being the victim.

As you journal your daily practice, remember to be honest in your reflections, thoughts, and conversations with your accountability partner. Create a practice that you can change when you are on the triangle. Infuse the practice with compassion and empathy so that you can stay off the Drama Triangle and move onto the Compassion Triangle. Write the change in your journal and ask your accountability partner to check in with you to see how things are going.

Continue to reflect on all of the daily practices and start to put the daily practices together as you move forward.

"
On tops of mountains,
as everywhere to hopeful souls,
it is always morning.
— Henry David Thoreau

Photo © Boris H. Pophristov

NORTH

US
395

>>

What would my life be like if I
were not using self-protective
behaviors and thoughts?

Photo © Erick Lohre

> "For true success ask yourself these four questions:
> Why? Why not? Why not me? Why not now?"
>
> —James Allen

Chapter 8

Self-Protective Systems

Self-protective systems for people are those default behaviors that are created over time and unconsciously used when similar stimuli come into our awareness. When I was a teenager and something happened that I did not like, I was very quick to blame the other person or in some way deflect responsibility. Acting as an emotionally charged victim meant that whatever happened to me was always someone else's fault. My self-protective default behaviors were to judge, blame, and shame the other person as much as I could. I was completely unaware that this was happening at the time. The connection to the triangle is that living life as a victim, persecutor, or rescuer also meant that I was

> **My self-protective default behaviors were to judge, blame, and shame the other person as much as I could.**

> **I used these strategies for survival to react to real and perceived threats in an instinctual or emotional fashion.**

creating default behaviors to go along with each category. I used these behaviors as my self-protective behaviors, and these behaviors protected me in interactions where I was emotionally charged.

I used these strategies for survival to react to real and perceived threats in an instinctual or emotional fashion—my go-to strategies were fight, flight, or freeze. I could have used reason to get through my interactions, but I was unable to use reason and plan my responses because I was unconscious. I was unable to reason because I was stuck in my automatic self-protective reactive behavior patterns. When I was in my self-protective behavior patterns, I was unconscious and unaware, and I thought the way I acted was normal.

My behaviors were learned after many years of a fight-or-flight environment in my home and in my head. After a period of time, the fight-or-flight thoughts and actions became hardwired into my head, and that was my normal. I lived my life self-protecting myself even when I had no reason for protection. I was so disconnected from being authentic that I could not recognize people who had my best interests at heart, so I treated them from my triggered victim place.

I was more concerned with my own ego and how other people saw me than with how my behavior affected the other person. My goal was to have people think of me as a good person even though I was fully acting from a lens of protection. From a lens of protection, I treated every interaction as though the other person was out to get me because I am a victim. I unconsciously used my self-protection behaviors in every interaction that I had with the other person.

> **My goal was to have people think of me as a good person even though I was fully acting from a lens of protection.**
>
> **From a lens of protection, I treated every interaction as though the other person was out to get me because I am a victim.**

The connection of self-protective systems to the Drama Triangle is that my self-protective systems had been designed based on my experiences in the drama that occurred over my lifetime. The drama and behaviors became default because I could drop into them and not even be aware that that was what I was doing. I was completely oblivious that I was in drama because drama was normal to me. Self-protections are built on being defensive and are the byproduct of real experiences that have occurred between another person and me. At some point in my life, these self-protective behaviors served me in that they kept

> **At some point in my life, these self-protective behaviors served me in that they kept something at bay that was hurtful to me.**

something at bay that was hurtful to me. I had no understanding that my unwillingness to deal with my own drama was the root of my self-protective behaviors.

The beginning of this self-protective process starts with an emotional charge where some outside stimulus comes in and gets me emotionally charged. From this charge comes the possibility of being triggered or thrown. Being thrown is a process where I get knocked off my balance or triggered due to an outside interaction. I have the possibility of getting triggered when people do not treat me how I think they should, or when I get restimulated from a past interaction. In my work with people and creating change, I get thrown when people tell me that they do not care about the other person or fixing their relationship. I get thrown because I believe that relationships matter and we should care about each other. One of the messages I received through my sister's death is that we should appreciate and care for each other and not be a negative influence in another's life.

When I was younger and got thrown, I dropped into a self-protective behavior of blaming the other person instantly. Today when I get thrown interacting with people who don't seem to care about others, I have an internal process to self-examine my own motives and responses. I take responsibility and approach the interaction differently.

I work to support people in building strong and honest relationships, and when they display that they do not care about the relationship, it throws me. I was facilitating a bias awareness workshop for a group from a central department and was thrown at the beginning and end of the session. The audience was a team from a district operations department. In the beginning, a person started shouting, "These are bad kids, and you need to believe us when we tell you these are bad kids, and what are you going to do about them? When we tell you we have bad kids, it is your job to do something about them." My colleague was facilitating and talked about how her grandson had been called a "bad kid" in his school. After grandma had taken some action, grandma realized that her grandson was not a bad kid; he was just stuck in a bad environment. After she moved him to a more supportive environment, her grandson began to thrive.

At the end of the day, the same person talked about the bad kids when I was facilitating. I was triggered and thrown because I could not believe that someone who works in education would think students were bad. When I was triggered, I went into my head

I had no understanding that my unwillingness to deal with my own drama was the root of my self-protective behaviors.

> **I have judgmental thoughts, and at this point in my life, I know I have a choice about how I want to respond. I have done and continue to do my own personal work, so I now know what happens to me when I become judgmental.**

and judged her and had a set of judgmental biases about what I thought of this person based on being triggered.

I had to figure out how to craft my own response. So I asked this question: "If you think our kids are so bad, why would you want to engage with them?" This is a question I ask many educators when they talk about how bad kids are and how they cannot teach them, drive them, feed them, etc. I know that I was not as eloquent as my colleague was, and I do know that I was honest about how I was feeling.

When you are thrown, triggered, unnerved, agitated, activated—choose any expressive word that describes you when you are caught off balance—it is important to be vigilant and aware. Before doing my personal work, I reacted badly and would go into victim/persecutor modes and do my best to hurt other people using my self-protective behaviors. I did not care how they felt; I just knew that I had to put them in their place, and I knew what that place was. I wanted them to know how wrong they were because I was using my self-protective behavior of intimidation and discrediting others.

I have judgmental thoughts, and at this point in my life, I know I have a choice about how I want to respond. I have done and continue to do my own personal work, so I now know what happens to me when I become judgmental. I am more thoughtful about making a response that will allow me to let go of the judgment and come back and be present.

> **I wanted them to know how wrong they were because I was using my self-protective behavior of intimidation and discrediting others.**

I had to figure out how to use my voice in a way that was firm and direct and did not allow any self-protective behavior to hijack my authenticity. Crafting my response when thrown is not about the other person as much as it is about enhancing my ability to speak my truth when I am thrown or triggered while accepting and owning my role in the interaction. Self-protective systems and behaviors are not designed to be the most productive way to move through life, because they're based on the past instead of the present, and it takes persistence to understand the role of self-protective behaviors in your interactions.

Before I became aware, my self-protective behaviors were the only way I knew to make myself feel that I had any power or control over what was going on. Self-protective thoughts and behaviors are often unconscious and deniable. When confronted by someone who made me mad, I would use a self-protective behavior of being defensive and would still deny that that was what I was doing. Being unaware of my self-protective behaviors meant that I did not have to own them or accept any responsibility for the relational outcome.

I had to start asking myself, what would my life be like on a daily basis if I were not using self-protective behaviors and thoughts? Who would I be without my guarded behaviors?

Think about the self-protective behaviors, thoughts, and strategies that you are using and the impact they are having in your life. Where are you stuck on the triangle, and how are your self-protective strategies supporting you in staying there? What are the messages you are giving yourself about your own lack of empowerment or victim mentality, and how are those messages connected to your self-protective behaviors?

Before I became aware, my self-protective behaviors were the only way I knew to make myself feel that I had any power or control over what was going on. Self-protective thoughts and behaviors are often unconscious and deniable.

Chapter 8 Daily Reflective Practice
Self-Protective Behaviors

Think about the following self-protective behaviors:

- ◆ Intimidation/domination
- ◆ Discrediting others' competence
- ◆ Blaming
- ◆ "I'll do it myself"/martyr
- ◆ Acting "politically"/being nice or tough
- ◆ Self-righteousness/making others wrong
- ◆ Making excuses
- ◆ Restricting the flow of information
- Withdrawal
- Cynicism and despair
- Self-sabotage
- Disempowering others
- Sarcasm
- Humor

♦ Intellectualization

♦ Acting confused

♦ Coalition building

♦ Others …

Take out your journal and create a list of self-protective strategies, behaviors, thoughts, and actions that are driving your life. Go back to the self-reflection assessment you did and think about the behaviors and outcomes you identified. In the previous practice, you looked at behaviors that caused drama and dropped you on the triangle. Where were you on the triangle, and what were the self-protective behaviors that you used? Reflect on how these self-protective behaviors have affected your life.

See if you can access 10 to 20 self-protective behaviors you have used and then prioritize them into the top five that you use the most. As part of the reflection, write down all the ways that you and your relationships are affected when you are in that self-protective behavior. What is the impact on your relationship? How do you feel during and after the interaction? Where were you on the triangle? After you have completed this process, think about one relational interaction that you want to change. Think about a person who has behaviors that cause you to get on the triangle. How can you use your awareness of self-protective behavior to stay off the triangle? Can you set up an interaction with that person to practice not dropping into the triangle and your self-protective strategy?

Work with your accountability partner and share one self-protective behavior you want to change to a strength and how you want to be held accountable. What are the daily practices you are going to use to change the narrative and behavior? What strategies are you going to use to heighten your self-awareness when you are getting on the Drama Triangle in order to enable yourself to move onto the Compassion Triangle? What strategies are you going to develop to get yourself off of the Drama Triangle? Work with your accountability partner to hold yourself accountable for the changes you want to make, and remember to be compassionate and empathetic to yourself. We will reconnect to this daily practice when we start to get into the conversations on bias.

The conversations on bias are at the heart of this work and are the place where you can find a way to understand, heal, let go, build nurturing relationships, and continue to move forward.

Photo © Erick Lohre

"
"As he thinks, so he is;
as he continues to think, so he remains."

—James Allen

Chapter 9

Conversations on Bias

All of the practices we have been talking about in the previous chapters lead us to the heart of the work being done for personal growth. The purpose of this book is to provide support in creating steps that enable you to make great strides in your personal growth through awareness, practice, and accountability. Bias awareness is the journey I have been on since age 18, and as a teenager, I could not name it as I started or when I was working through the process because I did not know that that was what I was doing. The understanding, acceptance, and normalizing of my own biases have given me the ability to grow and sustain that growth.

> **The point of this conversation is to practice engaging in a conversation about your own bias and see how deep the conversation will go. You need to give yourself 45 to 60 minutes for this conversation. It does not matter which bias you share; it matters only that you engage in the practice of the process.**

I have also learned to describe the process of bias awareness in the following way.

Each of us has unique preferences, perspectives, and ideas. The blend of our individuality creates an essential diversity, without which the world would be a bland place indeed. Our unique perspectives can also interfere with our ability to be impartial and unprejudiced. This leads to bias.

The primary bias awareness question is "Do my biases inhibit or enhance my ability to be in an authentic relationship?" Our biases can be the root of our thoughts and actions, yet we rarely talk about their impact on our decision making.

The discussion of bias is difficult because when we think of a biased person, we think of something negative like someone who is racist, bigoted, discriminatory, or prejudiced. When we view others through our preconceived notions and stereotypes, biases become a problem. The problem approach to bias awareness kept me stuck because I thought I was a bad person.

Bias, however, is a normal part of being human and is worth taking a look at, to preserve the health of our relationships, cultures, and communities. The approach to bias awareness is to continue to have the deeper conversations about our roots—biases—and their impacts on our behaviors, families, professions, and community.

The conversations on bias are at the heart of this work and are the place where you can find a way to understand, heal, let go, build nurturing relationships, and continue to move forward.

In the past, bias was regarded as abnormal, conscious, and intentional. But current research shows that bias is normal, unconscious, and mostly unintentional. It is possible to be aware of implicit attitudes and beliefs, and/or limit the effects of bias on our behavior. Human biases are malleable, and biased behaviors and judgments can be disrupted. Bias does not equal racist, sexist, or homophobic; bias equals being a normal human being.

◆ There is a level of cognitive dissonance with bias; cognitive dissonance is where our biases do not match our beliefs. A simple example of cognitive dissonance would be to ask you if you believe that texting while driving is harmful. Most of us would say yes, texting and driving is harmful. The follow-up question is, how many of you have texted while driving? A majority of people who think texting while driving is harmful have texted while driving. This is cognitive dissonance. Normalizing the bias conversation is about seeing yourself as a regular human being making sense of how we categorize our interactions.

Before we move into the bias conversation, I want you to reflect on the daily practices you have been using up to this point. Going back through the various chapters to review important points can help connect the dots. The bulleted list below shows where we have been. These are also the tools you will be using for the next process.

- Self-Assessment
- Why?
- Personal Agreements
- Origination Point
- Purposeful Conversations
- Deep Listening
- Drama Triangle
- Self-Protective Strategies

You created your Why so you could connect everything you do to your desired outcome. You created personal agreements to hold yourself accountable, and you conducted your self-assessment to reflect on your thoughts, behaviors, and actions when interacting in relationships.

We talked about the origination point of bias and how bias is introduced between birth and adolescence and how it carries into our adult interactions. We talked about how to have a purposeful conversation and to look at why the conversation is happening, what you want to accomplish through the conversation, how you measure success, and how you are facilitating the conversation.

The primary bias awareness question is "Do my biases inhibit or enhance my ability to be in an authentic relationship?"

The deep listening process was focused on presence and self-awareness, which enables you to be aware of whether you are reactive or responsive in conversation. Listening and being present for another person shows that you care about the other person and what they are saying. We stepped into the Drama Triangle to become aware of when we are on the triangle and how to stay out of drama and how to stay in compassion. We concluded with self-protective systems, and we are now moving into the conversations on bias.

Using all these tools will support you in the work of transforming the conversations on bias and uncovering the origination point(s) to create healing and understanding.

The ideal process for the conversation on bias is to work in a group of four people. I have tried various numbers, and four is helpful for the diversity of the conversation and to

> **The story of being worthless and that I would never amount to anything was very challenging to overcome. I could do things that I was not sure of and be sort of successful; all the while, the story in the back of my head was still circulating. I had to create a daily practice of replacing that negative message with a positive message that I was capable and able to be successful.**

facilitate deeper learning. If you are not reading with a group or doing a book study with your team, this conversation could happen between you and your accountability partner, or in an online format with our team.

The setup and the process are the same for two or four people. You start out by sitting in a small circle, with your chairs close enough so that you can almost touch knees. Next, take a moment to think about a bias you are willing to share with your small group. It is important to create an entry point to start the conversation. If you have enough trust in the group, you can go deeper. If you are getting to know each other, you may have to gradually work your way toward sharing from a deeper point in your story. The purpose of the entry point is that it allows everyone to be engaged in the conversations. Conversations on bias are not about sharing the right bias as much as they are about practicing talking about bias.

The process creates a personal entry point into the conversation for each person because it allows you to decide which bias you want to share. You can share something that has a huge charge for you or one with a small charge. I had a participant in a workshop who said, "I don't really trust everyone in this group, and I am not sure that I want to share." He did not feel comfortable sharing a deep personal bias. I went over to talk and asked if there was a bias he was willing to share, an experience or interaction that gets him emotionally charged. After a moment, he thought and said, "I hate the vegetable beets." Beets were an interesting thing to have a bias against, so I knew there was a story there. I asked if he would be willing to tell us the story of having a bias against beets, and this is the story he shared.

When he was 8 or 9 years old, his mother decided it was time for him to try beets. When he came home after school, the house smelled of beets, and it was a bad smell. When he was served beets, he refused to eat them, and his mother sat at the table with him for hours. This traumatic childhood interaction still triggered a negative restimulated experience for him. As an adult, when he encountered the smell of beets or someone eating beets, he would leave the room.

As this participant got closer to the origination point, he realized that the beet bias stemmed from a negative experience that had been imposed upon him as a child. He had been forced to do something he did not want to, and that had stuck with him into adulthood. His beet bias was his entry point into the group bias conversation.

When I came back to check in on the conversation after about 15 minutes, all four were fully engaged in the conversation, talking about more personal experiences that had happened within their family interactions. Had I told this person to share a specific personal bias, he probably would have checked out and not engaged in the conversation.

The point of this bias conversation is to practice engaging in a conversation about your own bias and to see how deep the conversation will go. You need to give yourself 45 to 60 minutes for this conversation. It does not matter which bias you share; it matters only that you engage in the practice of the process. Before you get into the bias conversations, let's add some more context to the approach.

The definitions that I am working with about bias are the following:

- ♦ Bias is simply each person's unique predisposition for how to see the world. It's our own thinking when we are confronted with new events.
- ♦ Bias is used to describe a tendency or preference toward a particular perspective, ideology, or result.

When you see these two definitions, they are not charged

either way. They do not say that bias is good or bad; they simply say that biases are created by an experience that we have, which we add meaning to. The research also shows that we all categorize and stereotype consciously or unconsciously in all of our interactions. In the story I told you about my dad, my categorization process was really simple: You are a man. My stereotype process was also very simple: All men are mean. I would then jump to a final meaning, because I had a preformed

> **The purpose of the entry point is that it allows everyone to be engaged in the conversations. Conversations on bias are not about sharing the right bias as much as they are about practicing talking about bias.**

negative opinion based on my past experience, and I would discriminate by treating a man I had just met according to my bias against men. This stereotype was an example of a preformed negative opinion or attitude toward a group of people based on characteristics such as race, religion, disability, sexual orientation, age, or ethnicity.

Once I had this preformed negative opinion, I would then discriminate by treating this man exactly as if he were my dad. Discrimination is a conscious choice that we don't want to be aware of because discriminating against each other does not feel good. In fact, I was discriminating, judgmental, and stereotyping this other man due to my bias.

> **I had to create a daily practice of replacing that negative message with a positive message, that I was capable and able to be successful.**

While my experience with my dad was real, he does not represent an entire group of men, so I had a lot of work to do. My bias against men completely inhibited my ability to be in authentic relationships with men for a long time. As a teenager, I would not trust men, even if they were nice to me, because my experience at home had been "I love you" one day and "I am going to beat you" the next. As I started doing this personal work, I learned that my dad was one person and did not represent all men. I had to deal with the biased experience that was not allowing me to be in an authentic relationship, and also the narrative that was given as a part of that experience.

The story of being worthless, and that I would never amount to anything, was very challenging to overcome. I could overcome physical challenges successfully while the story in the back of my head was still circulating, or so I thought. In reality, when I started this journey I was not very successful with changing my physical choices or the narrative that was in my head about not being successful.

I had to create a daily practice of replacing that negative message with a positive message, that I was capable and able to be successful. The entry point into this conversation is important, so think about a bias you are willing to share with your small group.

Finding an entry point and creating an entry point for others into this conversation is critical. For you and many other people, admitting that you have biases may be new, and I am sure sharing them with others is new. Using the personal agreements, especially the one regarding awareness of judgment that leads to blame or shame, is important. Be sure to reflect on your personal agreements. You may even want to print a copy and have it with you during the conversation. As you set up the bias conversation, you will want to be with your accountability partner, or partners, and form a group of four. When you are in your circle, the beginning process is to quickly go around the circle sharing your biases without the story.

The steps in the conversation on bias are the following:

Name a bias that you have. For example: "I have a bias toward bad drivers." All participants go around quickly and name the bias without

The story of being worthless, and that I would never amount to anything, was very challenging to overcome.

In reality, when I started this journey I was not very successful with changing my physical choices or the narrative that was in my head about not being successful.

any story: "My bias is … my bias is … my bias is …"

Once everyone in the group has shared a bias, it is time to start a conversation. One of the questions you will be answering is, "Do my biases inhibit or enhance my ability to be in authentic relationship?" This question allows you to start to think about the biased experience, the story you made about it, and the way the past biased experiences control your interactions in the present. Go ahead and quickly have each person share his or her bias.

The reason to initially quickly go around and say "My bias is …" is that you want to make sure everyone has the opportunity to share a bias. If you share the bias and then get right into the story before everyone has shared, you run the risk of some of the people in your circle not being able to share because of time. I would say, "I have a bias against people who drink because that was my experience with my dad." The bias against people who drink is how my bias was experienced as an adult. The reality of my bias when I get to the origination point story is that I have a bias against people who don't provide a loving and secure environment for their children.

Once everyone has shared a bias, then you can have a conversation and tell the story of your biased experience or ask a question of another person in the circle. I encourage you to use the purposeful conversation model combined with deep listening. Deep listen from the perspective of being present and not impassive so you can have a responsive, lively conversation. Stay aware of whether you are listening in a reactive or a responsive mode, with responsive listening being the place of deeper interaction. The point of this conversation is not to finish; it is to see how deep the conversation can go. The effort is to see if you can get to the origination point of the original biased experience through the conversation.

> **As you engage in a bias conversation, allow your feelings to surface and simply acknowledge that you are having an emotional reaction to your story. This is a normal part of the process.**

I had a group of participants at a half-day training in conversations on bias, and at the end, a person wanted to talk to me. She came up to me and said, "I think you just saved my marriage." This was a new statement for me after many years of facilitation with thousands of people, so I was quite interested in the story. She told me that through our work she had discovered something about the origination point of bias that was showing up in her life.

She had been married for four years, and she had a normal marriage with the usual relationship issues. She told me that over the past few months, she and her husband had had the most horrible arguments in their marriage because

> **Conversations on bias provide opportunities to normalize what you are feeling and create a process of introspection and healing.**

of a change in work schedule. Her husband had just switched jobs and had gone from working 30 to 40 hours a week at his previous job to a startup where he was now working 60 to 75 hours every week.

One of the results of the self-awareness with bias work is to get to the origination point of the biased experience. The origination point is the point of understanding and healing. If you can reach the origination point, change behaviors, and shift the story you made, the control that the bias has on your current interactions will lessen.

The participant told me that she had discovered, through our half-day training, the origination point of the current challenges with her husband. She said that when she was 12 years old, she had been abandoned. This was a part of her life that she had not shared with anyone, including her husband, and she had not done any healing because of the pain she had suffered as that 12-year-old abandoned girl.

What she realized is that when she was arguing with her husband about not being home, as a 35-year-old woman, she reverted into that hurt 12-year-old girl. She was bringing all of the emotionally charged, unhealed hurt into the interaction with her husband. The point of healing for her at 35 was to go back to the 12-year-old girl and start a healing process. From the origination point of understanding, she was able to start a healing process for herself and repair the relationship with her husband.

For you, the bias conversation provides the ability to normalize what you are feeling and create a process of introspection and healing if needed. As you engage in this conversation, allow your feelings to surface and just acknowledge that you are having an emotional reaction to your story. This is a normal part of the process. Remember not to get on the Drama Triangle as you share and hear other people in your group share their stories. You may get restimulated due to someone else's bias story and want to jump on the Drama Triangle. If you get on the Drama Triangle, accept it and see if you can move yourself to the Compassion Triangle. Understand that you may reflect a bias that another person is sharing and may drop into some level of judgment.

I was facilitating and participating in a bias circle when one of the participants pointed her finger at me and said, "You are my bias." I was instantly highly emotionally charged, and I had a lot of judgment going on in my head about her. I had just met this person and had no idea how I could be her bias. I was restimulated because I had been blamed in the past for hurting other people and had just started my own process of healing. As all this emotion and judgment was swirling in my head, I had a decision to make. I decided to sit quietly and listen to what happened next.

After an awkward silence, another person asked her if she knew me, and she said no. Another person asked her how someone she did not know could possibly be her bias. She told a story from her younger days about interacting with someone who looks like me and at the end said, "Someone who looks like you raped me." Had I just gone off on my emotionally charged, judgmental first reaction, I would have hurt her and reinforced the negative bias that men are jerks and you can add me to the list.

My being quiet allowed her to tell her story, and we connected after the session for more conversation. My hope is that through that interaction she was able to continue her healing process and see that not all men who reflect her bias are jerks.

Once you feel ready, start the bias conversation, and when it feels complete take some time to journal and reflect on the process and the feelings and thoughts that arose for you. Think about the origination point and then take the next step in your daily practice.

Chapter 9 Daily Reflective Practice
Bias Conversations

The purpose of this bias conversation is to remember that this work is about practice and not perfection. Once you have completed the bias conversation, take some time to journal about your experiences and feelings going through the conversation. Explore the feelings that come up for you and whether you become emotionally charged through the conversation. Did anyone in the circle get emotional? If so, what was your response to that expression of emotion? Continue to explore your biases and connect your bias to an emotional charge, and start to track what gets you emotionally charged throughout your day.

Think about whether you go to judgment of the person and blame him or her for what is happening. Or do you look within and think about what it is about you that believes the other person is not right or whatever other judgment you have? Journal your experiences and share them with your accountability partner. Bias awareness is a lifelong endeavor that can continue to support changes in your current interactions. The ultimate outcome is to use normalizing bias awareness conversations and actions as a tool for continued growth and understanding.

> Every act of a [person] springs from the hidden seeds of thought, and could not have appeared without them.
>
> James Allen

Photo © Will Dickey

"

"A person is limited only by the thoughts that he chooses."

— James Allen

Chapter 10

Next Steps

Once you have completed the conversations on bias, it is time to debrief your experience. I always ask a couple of questions to everyone after the bias conversations. The first question is, "Did you learn anything new about anyone in your circle?" The second question is, "Did you find that you had a shared bias with anyone in your circle?" You may not have told them you had a shared bias, so reflect on this shared bias question.

For question 1, typically 100 percent of the room finds that they learned something new about the other person because, for many in the bias conversation, this is the first time they have shared bias stories. The second question usually gets

> **Authentic relationships matter, and each of us has the power to make real connections with each other that are based on truth and not judgment, relationships that are based on authentic interactions and not made-up stories.**

between 80 to 100 percent of the people to raise their hands, and I follow this up with another question: "If we have so many shared biases, why are we so afraid to talk about them?"

The first question is about taking the time to develop deeper relationships with the people in our lives whom we care about, whether they are in our personal or professional life. Some days I spend more time with the people I work with than my own family, so having healthy relationships at work is important. The intent of creating a deeper relationship is getting to know each other beyond name and title. There is so much more to each of us beyond name and title, and having intentional time to get to know each other matters. One area where I believe it is important is something I caused a lot of during the first half of my life and an area that I now spend time supporting people to move through: conflict.

Take a moment to reflect on some of the best relationships you have today. These could be a significant other, sibling, best friend, children, or anyone else you love and care about. When you are in a conflict with these people, you are probably more willing to apologize, push the conversation, own your role, or let something go, because the relationship means more to you than being mad at that person. Imagine the kind of communities, workplaces, and world we could live in if the relationships mattered more than staying mad at the other person. Imagine the world we would live in if we could all resolve our conflicts at the lowest level, which is person to person.

Authentic relationships matter, and each of us has the power to make real connections with each other that are based on truth and not judgment, relationships that are based on authentic interactions and not made-up stories. Being authentic starts with getting to know yourself and being willing to look within to see what your biases are and how they are affecting your relationships. With conscious bias awareness, you will be able to realistically assess your interaction in relationships from an authentic perspective. Through authenticity, you and the other person can decide how deep you want to take the relationship.

The second question is wrapped around the notion of why we are afraid to talk about biases if we have so many that are shared. I want you to think about the personal agreements that we created at the beginning of this book and reflect on this question: "Which personal agreement do you think was most at play that allowed you to be self-reflective throughout your bias conversation?"

If you answered the one that says awareness of judgment that leads to blame or shame, then you are correct. With that one working agreement, you knew that you could say whatever you wanted to say throughout the bias conversations. You knew that no matter what you said, no one was going to judge, blame, or shame you for what you shared.

Imagine the difference in our conversations if we were able to treat each other with that one working agreement. Awareness of judgment that leads to blame or shame has the ability to shift our conversations. Instead of having conversations about who, we would be talking about what, and how do "we" fix it. Imagine how authentic your interactions will be if you can give yourself an awareness of self-judgment that leads to no self-shame or self-blame. With awareness and actions, you can give these personal agreements to yourself and support your constant growth and development.

If we have so many shared biases, why are we so afraid to talk about them?

Conclusion

This has been quite a journey, and if you have stayed committed to the daily practices, you are seeing and feeling shifts and changes in how you approach life. Remember that this work is about practice and not perfection, so continue to find opportunities to practice. When you started reading this book, it was wrapped around finding the steps to grow from where you are to where you want to be. This work is daily, and you must be vigilant moving forward to make sure that you do not backslide. When you do backslide and become judgmental or recognize a bias, be kind, compassionate, and loving to yourself. I started my journey at 18, and it will be a constant in my life until the day I stop breathing.

Think about the good fruits of character to employ: kindness, gentleness, patience, faithfulness, self-control, goodness, and joy … the love of self and our neighbors.

Remember to ask yourself, "Do my biases inhibit or enhance my ability to be in an authentic relationship?" If your biases inhibit your ability to be in an authentic relationship, what is the work you need to do for yourself? You no longer have to move through life being a victim and allowing other people to dictate how you feel or respond. If you get stuck or slip, go back and reread the chapter connected to what you want to change … and grow and change. Check in with your accountability partner frequently and hold yourself accountable for staying in awareness and moving to action.

This work I have shared with you has been the most rewarding work I have done in my life, and the practices have become second nature after having done them for so long. I have to remain vigilant because I still surface implicit bias, and I don't ever want to put myself into such an egotistical place that I convince myself that I am there and done with my work. Complacency is the root of denial and unconscious behavior.

I believe that normalizing conversations on bias is a path that will support us to be more compassionate and care for each other. Stay awake, stay aware, and grow fully into the person you were put on the planet to be, because we all need what you have to offer.

"

Do my biases inhibit
or enhance my ability
to be in an authentic
relationship?

Photo © Erick Lohre

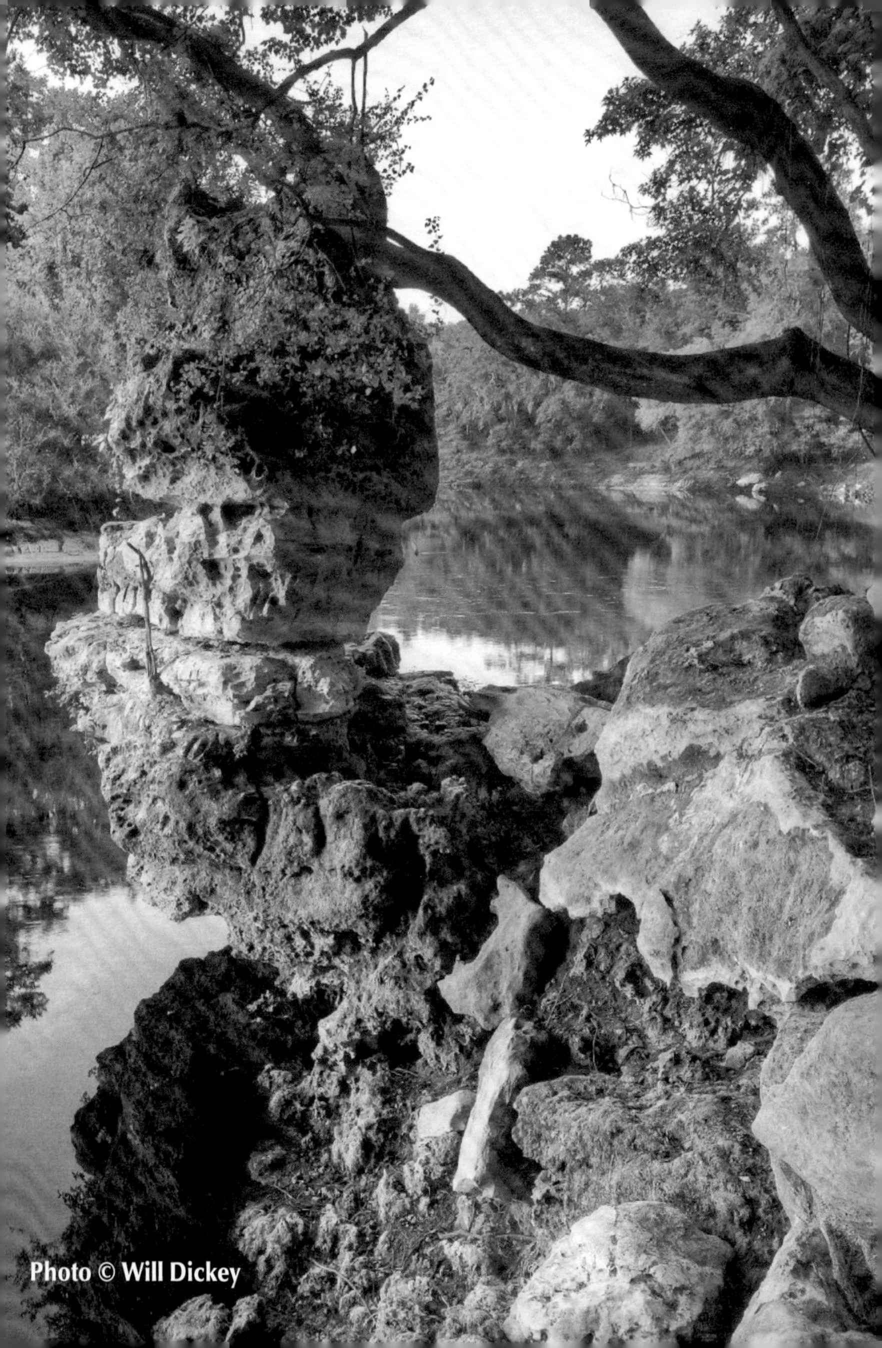

Photo © Will Dickey

"

"As a person thinketh in his heart, so shall he be."

— James Allen

Appendix

My Results

Over the past 40 years, I have read many self-help books that told me what I needed to do to change without adding the steps or actions needed to change. When I would get to the end of the book, I often wondered what happened to the author. Did the authors use the same practices from their books for personal growth? If they did use them, how were they successful, and what are the personal changes that have been made? I wanted to share with you the changes I have made using the techniques in this book to make and sustain personal growth.

I am going to use my initial personal assessment. In my assessment, the answers are reflective of where I was when

Daily Reflective Practice #1

Self-assessment of my own thoughts, behaviors, and actions

My Thought	My Behavior
People make me mad.	Standoffish—Not willing to get to know others
No one has the ability to make me mad unless I choose to be.	Open to getting to know other people for who they are
Judging other people	Do not allow people to get close; think the worst of them
Everyone is unique and has something to offer.	Am aware of my judgment and can put judgment aside to remain present
I am a victim of other people's actions.	I behave as though other people can make me feel happy, sad, and the like through their actions.
I will accept and own the impacts of my behavior.	I control how I face my day, and no one has the ability to make me feel an emotional response unless I choose to.
I will never be successful.	I take on things that I know nothing about to prove that story wrong.
I have everything I need to grow into the person I am meant to be.	**My story is about being present and living in the moment and allows the authentic interactions to unfold.**
The world revolves around me.	I do things that give me titles or perceived power.
The world is evolving, and I am bearing witness to the amazing changes in our communities.	I do things that elevate others and show them their strength.

Daily Reflective Practice #1, continued
Self-assessment of my own thoughts, behaviors, and actions

My Action	Outcome
Interactions that don't go well	Negative relationships
Interactions that I let evolve without expectations	More authentic interactions with less conflict
Don't expose or open myself to others	No trust in others or myself to build relationships
Am willing to be myself most of the time in my interactions	Allow others to be trustworthy and to trust myself and my intuition
I act sullen or disconnected until other people show me that they have my best interests at heart.	Disappointment because my expectations were not met and I continued distrust of people
I am excited to meet new people and interact with them authentically.	I trust that others care and deserve trust. Loss of expectations so that I am always surprised and never disappointed.
I say yes to things that I don't know about and do not always follow through to completion.	People lose faith in me, and I become resigned to the fact that I don't have what it takes to be successful in life.
I have areas of expertise that I focus on. I want to always be curious and learn new things.	People engage in the work with me, and I use all my tools for success. Daily vigilance is required, and I am willing to give intention and vigilance to myself.
I get involved in projects that elevate my ego by title or role.	I am never satisfied with where I am and am constantly searching for more.
I am humbly, intentionally, and empathetically involved in projects that are connected to my Why.	I am not complacent and am always looking for opportunities to make the world a more humane place. I am happy and at peace with who I am.

I started this journey in 1975. I have attached my first assessment answers, and I want to add an explanation about the changes I have made with 42 years of daily practice.

The graph reflects the first assessment that I did about my thoughts, behavior, actions, and outcomes when I started my journey in 1975. The bolded set of reflections is where I am today after using the strategies and processes in this book.

Using the tools I have shared enables me to continue to grow and evolve as a person. I am not perfect, and I'm not striving for perfection. I am striving to be the very best version of myself that I can be each and every day. I will continue to use these tools daily to remain aware of what is happening in my interactions and to take responsibility for the outcomes.

Years ago, I was in an argument with my wife, and I dropped into my ego self. I told her I could not understand why she would not just get over it, forgive me, and move on. She looked at me and said with certainty and clarity, "Don't ever rush my process." Those words have stuck with me. Wherever you are in your process is where you need to be. Don't rush your process. Take your time and be gentle and honest with yourself as you strive to be the very best version of yourself you can be. I hope that the tools in this book can propel you toward your most powerful and authentic destiny.

My greatest wish is that the strategies I have shared here will have a positive impact on the lives of each of you reading this and that your life be one of great fulfillment and courage.

Glossary

Bias—A preconceived tendency or inclination to see people and situations with a defined, preconceived filter, which is often inflexible and negative. Biases prevent us from experiencing people and situations from a more neutral and authentic viewpoint.

Bias Conversation—A conversation designed to support participants in openly sharing a bias in order to help acknowledge biases, and to help normalize and promote openly talking about biases with other people.

Compassion Triangle—A psychological concept developed and diagrammed by Dr. Stephen Karpman depicting interactive roles in relationship, designed to support people in using compassion to move themselves off the Drama Triangle.

Deep Compassionate Listening—The process of being fully and compassionately present while listening without distraction. Thich Nhat Hanh states that this type of listening can help relieve the suffering of others.

Drama Triangle—Created by Dr. Stephen Karpman, depicting a psychosocial model of human interaction. It shows the destructive interactions that can occur between people when in conflict.

Origination Point—The place in time when an experience led to the creation of a bias. Understanding your origination points can help lead to understanding and healing.

Self-Protective Behaviors—Self-protective behaviors are reactive behaviors originally created from painful experiences and are designed to protect us from emotional harm. Maintaining self-protective behaviors keeps us stuck in dysfunctional patterns focused on the past rather than the present.

Restimulated Emotional Experience—An unhealed negative experience that gets retriggered in current relationships and interactions. They will often continue to negatively affect current interactions until the original experience is acknowledged and healed.

Wherever you are in your process is where you need to be. Don't rush your process. Take your time and be gentle and honest with yourself as you strive to be the very best version of yourself you can be.

Andrew Kowalyshyn, akphoto.com

About the Author

Author Bill de la Cruz is an inspiring leader who has been guiding individuals and groups through the process of personal transformation as a mediator and workshop leader for 30 years. He developed his programs and workshops in order to help individuals and groups build self-awareness and enhance relationships, and to help foster positive, sustainable personal growth. Bill has been on his own personal growth journey for more than 40 years, which inspired him to develop specific practices designed to help create positive, lasting change.

This book grew out of Bill's personal experience attending hundreds of self-help trainings and reading hundreds of self-help books. Many of these experiences told him that he must do "the work," but they too often failed to clearly define what that work should actually look like. Out of this 40-year journey, Bill developed daily practices that continue to support his personal growth and self-awareness, and he has dedicated himself to making these practices available to others.

Bill works on the Culture, Equity, and Leadership Team (CELT) at a large urban school district using these techniques to support personal and organizational change.

He is currently the Director of Equity and Inclusion with Denver Public Schools (DPS). DPS is the largest urban school district in the state of Colorado, with a student population of more than 90,000 and 15,000 employees. Bill works on a team responsible for developing and facilitating equity- and inclusion-infused leadership development in the district. The approach is designed to create systems and cross-functional cultures that are collaborative using personal relationships as the vehicle for change.

Bill lives in Denver, Colorado, with his wife, Lora. He has four children, Sophie, Joey, Savana, and Zack, and a grandson, Jackson.

Bill continues to conduct a variety of personal growth, business communication, and relationship-enhancing workshops for companies and groups in Colorado and nationwide and can be reached at b.delacruz@comcast.net.

Testimonials

As a teacher, it is often difficult to take a day away from the classroom; however, this training went far beyond my expectation and has reinvigorated and made me feel excited to go to school today.

—Angie Brown, MA, *Special Education*

When I first landed in the same school district as Bill, his Foundational Bias Training was one of my first professional development experiences. I knew in that training I had landed in the right school district. I am a better-equipped educator and a more caring person because of Bill's ongoing presence in my professional life.

—Michael P. Lovett, MA

Bill's training and guidance around cultural responsiveness has allowed me to recognize my own bias, improve communications, and effectively lead my teachers and students through a new lens on the world around me. I am forever grateful for the growth this training has inspired in me.

—Erin Dreeszen, *Instructional Leadership Team Partner*

I've been able to get a closer look at experiences in life that have forged opportunities to look at my own biases and how they impede growth. Your work gives space, time, and setting to power up without the excess junk of shame and blame. Thank you, brother!

—Sylvia Bookhardt, *Mentor for Leaders of Color*

" "

After engaging in my
own work for a number
of years, I figured out
that there were daily
practices to change
my thinking and
behaviors. I now take
the approach that
thinking and behaviors
can be changed with
commitment and
practice.

Acknowledgments

I want to thank my family for supporting me in writing this book and for being my accountability partners in this journey. My beautiful wife, Lora, held me accountable, put up with my growth challenges, and pushed me when needed especially to complete this book. My children, Sophie, Joey, Savana, and Zack, challenged me to look at myself in ways of parenting that pushed me to grow in ways I never could have imagined. My family stuck with me in the darkest part of my changes, supported me in ways that I needed to be pushed, and continues to love and support me.

My cousins Andi and John, who in 1979 took me in when a one-month stay in Colorado turned into a year and who supported me in getting settled in Colorado. My brother, Richard, and my sister Kathy, who lived through many of the same experiences I share in this book. They have both found new ways to be in the world, and we have created new and loving relationships with each other. I want to thank Dr. Karpman, who allowed me to use his Drama Triangle to tell my story. I also want to thank and apologize to the many people who were part of my positive and negative experiences and relationship growth over the past 42 years. I continue to grow and appreciate all of the lessons I have learned and will continue to grow through all of the interactions I have.

> Man's mind may be likened to a garden, which may be intelligently cultivated or allowed to run wild.
>
> — James Allen